Making the Timeless Word Timely
A Primer for Preachers

Michael B. Brown

Smyth & Helwys Publishing, Inc.
6316 Peake Road
Macon, Georgia 31210-3960
1-800-747-3016

The paper used in this publication meets the minimum requirements of
American National Standard for Information Sciences—
Permanence of Paper for Printed Library Materials.
ANSI Z39.48–1984. (alk. paper)

Library of Congress Cataloging-in-Publication Data

Brown, Michael B., 1949-
Making the timeless Word timely : a primer for preachers / by Michael B. Brown.
pages cm
ISBN 978-1-57312-660-1 (pbk. : alk. paper)
1. Preaching. 2. Sermons, American. I. Title.
BV4211.3.B76 2013
251--dc23

2012047578

I dedicate this book to my former professor and lifelong friend,
Dr. James M. (Mickey) Efird,
who helped me understand that the Bible is not simply a spiritual
tome but also a pertinent and personal love letter from God to us

and also to cherished worshipers in Randleman, Welcome,
Stallings, Boone, Asheville, Winston-Salem, and New York,
who, in their faithful listening, have inspired me to remain
faithful in preaching.

Contents

Preface

It took me years to learn how to do what I do. In truth, I am still learning. My fear is that two weeks after I retire, I will have the ultimate epiphany and finally "get it."

However, I have been working at this craft as a full-time practitioner since June 1974. That constitutes a lot of Sundays; ergo, a lot of sermons. Through the years, I have come to understand (a) how simple the formula for successful preaching really is and (b) how challenging it is to produce an acceptable product week by week.

In relation to that first issue, the simplicity of homiletics, as a politician once said in a public speech: "It's really not rocket surgery." I love gaffes except when I make them. We know what he intended. What he said is more amusing. The truth is, when it comes to sermon preparation, it really is not rocket science (or brain surgery, take your pick). There is a simple formula for sermon preparation that creates messages that apply and engage whether your parish is rural or urban, young or old, rich or poor, five thousand members or fifty. It actually does not matter as far as "step one" is concerned. After this many years in ministry, and after having preached in small country parishes, large downtown congregations, university chapels, and civic centers, I now realize there is a method of sermon preparation that virtually without fail fits all sizes.

With regard to the second issue, the challenge of homiletics, this is where the preacher must employ the right side of the brain. This is the hard work. And we are talking about real work. Challenging work. Long work. Part of this task is to be creative and insightful enough to know how to take the general formula for sermon preparation (preparation, by the way, means *work*) and make it particular in its impact on a specific congregation. As the old adage goes, "Our task is to take the timeless Word and make it timely."

This book is succinct. It doesn't contain nearly as many pages as *War and Peace*. You can easily find a spot for it on your bookshelf. This is because what I have to say is simple. It is not simplistic, but it is simple. So even though we professional preachers are, by our very DNA, "wordy," this little treatise will economize on words. Hopefully, however, it will not economize on helpfulness. And perhaps it will ultimately help many of you discover some secrets of sermon preparation far earlier in the game than I did. Such, at least, is my reason for writing.

We will endeavor herein (a) to learn a consistently effective approach to constructing a sermon and (b) to acknowledge what it takes to employ that formula with integrity and excellence.

Thanks for reading!

—MB

CHAPTER 1

The Formula: Engage

To make them listen, first you have to get their attention. Entertainers understand this. They realize an audience must be engaged before it can appreciate the material presented. Homileticians speak to audiences. Thus, the same rule applies. If we do not engage the listeners at the outset, it is unlikely that they will tune in as the message progresses, just as few persons attending the theater decide to start paying attention to the play at the opening of act 2.

As a very young child, one of my sons realized that he could chatter away endlessly, but if I was not looking at him, he may or may not actually be "heard." So he would take my face in his hands, turn me in his direction, and then begin to speak. Only when I was properly focused did he share that which he felt a need to communicate. Similarly, only when a congregation is properly focused will it hear what we feel called to communicate. Therefore, the introduction of a sermon is a vital component of the whole. Its worth simply cannot be overemphasized.

How, therefore, do we grab the ear of the audience? There are numerous answers to that question, all effective in their own ways. One method of seizing the attention of an audience is through the use of humor. Many ministers are nervous about this, defensively retorting, "I'm not a comedian. And the Christian faith is far too important to turn into a punch line." I agree. But it is also far too important to be made boring. An appropriate amusing story that segues naturally into the text and theme of the day can get listeners on board as quickly as any other method. In so doing, it does not trivialize the gospel, but rather opens the ears of the audience.

Whereas some maintain that humor must always flow out of the personal experience of the preacher and must never be a traditional joke with a punch line, in truth that is not a concern worthy of your time. The issue is not whether the preacher was actually present when the parrot said, "Tell me, what did that chicken in the freezer do?" The important thing is that the congregation is listening intently to the unfolding of a story. They are hooked. They are engaged. They are present to the preacher. And the opening story opens their ears for hearing *the* story.

I have found that my congregation listens just as closely when I say, "Rita Rudner tells of a woman who . . ." as they do when I say, "I once met a woman who . . ." It really does not matter. What matters is that the story amuses them, which by definition means that it gets their attention. They follow the flow of the story to its conclusion, whether that is a formal punch line or a personal observation. They are in the moment. And, at the close of the moment, I have their attention as I begin to explore themes that are biblical, pastoral, and transformational. To feed their minds and souls, first we have to get their attention.

It is absolutely imperative, however, that the opening story indeed be *introductory*. Anything less than that compromises the integrity of the preaching event. The story must be a front porch that is attached to the actual house you wish the people to enter. A random funny story that has nothing to do with text or theme may well seize the audience's attention, but as the sermon progresses, its impact will be more confusing than informative. "Why did he begin with that joke?" "What does her funny story have to do with this biblical lesson?" Rest assured, once people are mentally wrestling with those questions, they are no longer paying proper attention to the message before them. Humor is a wonderful vehicle, but it has to take the audience in the direction the text itself demands that they go. A funny story cannot stand on its own. If disconnected from the day's primary theme, it will serve more to distract than to edify.

> A child approached a minister at the close of a service of worship. The child held out a quarter and said, "I want you to have this." The minister was puzzled. The child continued, "I kept this out of my lunch money from school. I thought you would need it." The minister replied, "Why do you think I need your money?" The second-grader responded, "Because you are poor." The minister smiled and said, "Where on earth did you get an idea like that?" to which the child answered, "My daddy told my mommy that you are the poorest preacher he ever heard!"

That is a funny story. It is the kind of story that gets the attention of an audience. However, on the heels of that story must come a statement like, "That must be how Paul felt when he learned that some of the church members in Corinth had pledged their allegiance to Peter, others to Apollos, and others to almost anyone except him. He had somehow landed on their 'poor preachers' list."

Could you use that story, however, to begin a sermon born of Paul's letter to the Galatians? The answer, obviously, is no. Why not? After all, Paul was not as popular there as he had been in Corinth. Why would it not be an acceptable use of humor as the introduction to a sermon from that epistle? The reason is that in Corinth there was a debate about which clergy was most and least effective. With the Galatians, though, there was simply a resistance to the message itself, not to a particular messenger. Thus, the line "You're the poorest preacher he ever heard" would be inconsistent when referring to a community that basically held all preachers in equal disregard. Let me reiterate: the point of an introductory story is not to amuse but rather to segue authentically into the text, being consistent with the text and not in any way distracting from the text.

Consider one other observation about the use of humor as in introductory tool. Even as you seek to make it pertinent, try also to make it fresh. At this point, the Internet is not our friend. By the time you run across that hilarious new anecdote on Google, half your congregation has read it as well. So beware of stories that are stale and overly familiar. Do I use them sometimes? Yes, but only with the disclaimer at the front, "I suspect many of you have heard this. It's been around a while. But it still sets the stage for what we want to say. A preacher, a banker, and a doctor decided to form their own company . . ." At least if I confess at the beginning that the story is familiar, there will not be as much eye-rolling when the first line is spoken. Even so, when it comes to humorous stories, fresh is better than stale and new is better than old. (Never—repeat, *never*—tell the story of the little boy looking at the memorial plaques in the narthex of the church and asking the pastor which service they died in, 8:45 or 11:00. Every human on planet earth has heard that story nine times. It's done. Find a new one.)

Whereas, as previously observed, it really doesn't matter whether a story is a traditional joke with a punch line or a personal experience, it is undeniable that a personal experience meets the "fresh" criterion in a way no packaged joke can. No one else has had the particular experience you are about to relate. No one has yet put it on a joke list on the Internet. It is your story. It belongs to you. You can weave the tale as you wish, and no one in the congregation has heard it before. Case in point: when I first moved to New York City, we had temporary housing in a lovely neighborhood called Murray Hill. Prior to our move, I had been in NYC only a few times and always as a tourist. Everyone knows Greenwich Village or Little

Italy, but most of us are not familiar with some of the less-famous neighborhoods in the city. So one Sunday morning I shared with our congregation an experience that was totally mine. It was not on the Internet because I was the person to whom it happened. It was not public property. The native New Yorkers loved it.

> Sometimes it's important to realize that we do not know as much as we think we do. Mark Twain was correct when he observed that we are all ignorant, just about different subjects. My ego was adjusted soon after moving here when I was in a lovely little market at the corner of Lexington and 34th. I was waiting in line to pay for a purchase. A friendly, chatty woman was in line behind me, and at one point she said to me, "Don't you just love Murray Hill?" I responded, "I'm sorry. I don't know who he is."

That story will not play well in Peoria, but it works for people who live in my city, and it's a story they have not heard before. Enough said. Just try to use humor that fits the text and is not so overused that it is counterproductive (remember, you are trying to engage the listeners, not sedate them). And don't forget that humor is merely a means, not an end in itself. If the people simply longed to hear a comedian, they would buy tickets to see Robin Williams. Instead, they have come to hear a theologian and biblical interpreter. The humor leads into the corpus of the message. Otherwise, it detracts from your purpose as a preacher.

Obviously, there are numerous ways to capture the attention of listeners, humor being only one method among many. Another is to quote someone who possesses status with the audience. In my church, ears still perk up when I begin by saying, "I was listening to a taped sermon by Norman Vincent Peale last week. He made a statement from this very pulpit fifty years ago, and it's still as meaningful today as it was then. Dr. Peale said . . ." In our context, his name has status, influence, and is instantly recognized. His statue stands beside our front doors on Fifth Avenue. His legacy saturates the building. So people listen when his name is quoted. To do so every week would soon become predictable and lose its impact, but to do so once every six months from this pulpit is a sure way to get the listeners' attention.

Wherever you are minister, one of your predecessors was your Dr. Peale. Someone who came before you was considered heroic. Do not be threatened by his or her memory. Instead, this can become a great tool in your preaching if you employ it sparingly and with obvious respect. Any minister at Riverside Church in New York City knows how easy it is to seize the audience's attention simply by referring to Fosdick, Coffin, or Forbes.

Certain names have indisputable status wherever one preaches. "Mother Theresa was so frank when she said . . . ." "At a retirement dinner in his honor, Billy Graham told the story of . . . ." "When he was still a young and privileged man and very much afraid of people who were different, St. Francis of Assisi one day turned a corner and found himself face-to-face with . . . ." "Knowing the risks and dangers involved, I doubt I would have had the courage to stand and speak as did Martin Luther King that day in . . . ." The mere mention of certain people will cause the majority of Christian audiences to tune in. In most churches, particularly those with even modest levels of theological sophistication, the circle of names is larger. One can mention Frederick Beuchner, Henri Nouwen, John Spong, Barbara Brown Taylor, Fulton J. Sheen, etc., and there is immediate recognition within the congregation.

There are, of course, names that are particular to specific demographics of the church and not so familiar to others. Any United Methodist congregation recognizes the name John Wesley (or the simple reference, "Wesley used to teach that . . ."). If that is not a familiar name in a Methodist church, then that congregation has not been paying attention to its unique history. However, when quoting Wesley to a congregation of the Reformed Church in America, I first have to explain briefly who the man was and why his teaching matters. All Protestants should recognize references to Luther without any mentoring. However, in a post-Boomer, contemporary Christian congregation, or even a megachurch led by a television personality/evangelist, it cannot be safely assumed that all listeners have the sufficient ecclesiastical memory to make the connection. (You do not want to be laboring to make a significant point while your hearers are asking themselves, "Luther who?")

Obviously, the names of countless nonchurch personalities have instant familiarity and, often, credibility. In most congregations, it is safe to assume there will be immediate recognition of names ranging from Ghandi to Michael Jordan, from Meryl Streep to Beyoncé. There are scores of names that prompt audiences to listen.

The same rule applies to quotes from or stories about notable personalities as it does to the use of humor: a quote or story must apply specifically to that which is to come next, that which is the corpus of the sermon. I may read a fabulous story about Oprah or Jimmy Carter, or hear a powerful statement attributed to Muhammad Ali or Helen Keller. It may be the most intriguing tale or the most inspiring quote imaginable. However, as an introduction to a sermon, the story or quote cannot stand on its own merit. In truth, if used as a sermon introduction, an anecdote has no merit of its own aside from that of being an engaging bridge to the real message. It is the text and application of the text that matter. The introduction, as previously observed, is the front porch. The real living occurs inside the house.

Personal stories are frequently excellent ways to perk the ears of an audience. "When I was a little girl, I spent my summers on my grandparents' farm in Iowa. On that farm was a handyman named Ben. I recall . . . ." "I was standing on a subway platform last week, waiting for the train, when I spotted . . . ." "Do you ever accidentally eavesdrop in a restaurant? It's not that you intend to overhear a conversation. It's rather that you can't miss what is being said. Recently I was having lunch at a little café near my home. Two well-dressed businessmen were seated at the table beside me. One said to the other . . . ." "Do you remember where you were on 9/11? I'll never forget where I was, or how I felt when I heard the news. Several friends and I were having a late breakfast at . . . ." "I had a birthday last week. Instead of receiving gifts, I asked each of my children to write me a poem. Well, our twelve year old daughter . . . ." "Last Saturday I was at a Duke basketball game. The man seated beside me was wearing a Gonzaga sweatshirt. I asked him . . . ." And off we go, telling a personal story that paints a word picture. The listener is invited into our world, to briefly share our experience. It is warm and welcoming. It is not yet a journey into deep biblical or theological waters. It has the feel of a Garrison Keillor report from Lake Wobegon.

There are numerous ways to begin a sermon. Harry Emerson Fosdick used to state his thesis in the first sentence so the listener would know what was about to be taught. Then he and the listener would explore that thesis together. I have colleagues who from time to time begin sermons by singing a stanza from a hymn. (My congregation offers financial perks to me if I promise never to be heard singing in public. Thus do I envy some of my friends who are blessed with melodious voices.) There are times when the employment of poetry captures attention beautifully, although in sermon introductions (as opposed to other parts of the message) this should only be done by memory. In the introduction, you want to engage the audience, which is rarely accomplished by limiting eye contact by reading. References to current events in the news are obviously timely and can be singularly helpful. The same is true of references to local community or congregational events. The point is to immediately seize the attention of the audience. How many important theological or pastoral presentations have fallen on deaf ears because the preacher's first sentence was, "The Greek word that Paul employed when talking about salvation was *soteria*, and in the Greek lexicon we read that . . ."? You might as well be speaking in Greek.

Sample Sermon Introductions

Let's take a look at a few introductory statements from preachers of note. Consider how their imagery and language connected with the world of their listeners, immediately creating a preacher/listener ambiance that was not so much "presentation" as "conversation" (i.e., a stylistic approach that turns "monologue" into "dialogue").

> I love the aroma of coffee as it is being brewed. Frequently on Sunday mornings about the time I am ready to stand and preach I can catch a whiff of the coffee brewing downstairs in the choir room as it wafts its way up the organ stairwell. I confess some mornings I would love to bolt down there, grab a cup, then race to the pulpit. I don't suppose many of you would notice. Often during weekday afternoons in the office, someone will brew a fresh pot of coffee and its aroma fills the whole office. Randy Newton will occasionally visit our offices bringing us experimental seasonal lattes he is testing for the Cove Coffeehouse. He is doing market research, but we enjoy being his test group.
>
> I remember early morning coffees and walks with students at youth camps and adults at family camps. The caffeine and company both stimulated those times. Coffee and conversation go together. A clergy friend in Oregon, John Evans, introduced me to a shot of espresso in coffee years ago. We were walking on a cold winter day in Seattle. That drink raised my blood pressure and my walking rate. It had punch.
>
> There are scriptures which are warm and soft. There are others that are beautiful, soaring and imaginative. There are passages which give wonderful glimpses of the grand transcendence of God. Our two passages today aren't in those groupings. Both of these passages are like

strong coffee, they have punch. So I invite you to think with me about "a triple espresso faith."[1]

Then the preacher launched into a consideration of Jesus' parable of the talents in Matthew and Paul's call to accountability and action in 1 Thessalonians. He carefully exegeted the meaning of "talents" (*denarii*) in Matthew's Gospel and the context in which Paul's audience would have read his words. All the while, one had in mind the energy that you feel after a shot of espresso, the energy that calls you to movement. The introduction painted a word picture that is vivid for the listeners and yet one which served simply as entrée to the biblical passages to be considered.

Every year I find a profound sense of hope in the president's State of the Union address, and this past Wednesday night was no different. It doesn't matter what party the president belongs to, or whether he has a gift for words or not. It is one of those occasions when the president— Democrat or Republican—is mostly at his best. Because on that night it seems all presidents try to do the same thing. They frame the particulars of their agenda and their assessment of where we are as a nation—all of which you may agree or disagree with depending on your politics—in a broader context that resonates with our deepest hopes and aspirations as a people. Most presidents on that night try to paint a portrait of what our best selves looks like: working across partisan lines for the good of all, compassion for the least among us, and concern about the welfare of the rest of the world.

Usually there are several ordinary Americans invited to sit up near the first lady, whose stories of extraordinary courage and self-sacrifice on behalf of fellow citizens are highlighted. It's always a speech that tries to lift us up out of our life-choking divisions, prejudices, cynicism, mean-spirited political accusations, score-keeping, and narrow self-interests. But as we know all-to-well, appeals for joining hands across our divides for the common good where the needs of all are considered are too often met by partisan ears in both the House chamber and living rooms across the land. The casting of lofty expansive visions is met with exclusive, narrow, and self-interested protests. By the end of the president's address, some folk are actually enraged. It happens every year regardless of what party occupies the White House.

For two Sundays now we've been listening to Jesus give a sort of combined inaugural/State of the Union sermon in his home-town synagogue at Nazareth. He's come to launch his public ministry.[2]

This sermon was preached at the National Cathedral in Washington DC. What a perfect engaging of the audience, most of whom had heard and many of whom had been present to hear the president speak at the State of the Union Address only four days earlier. Additionally, it was worded in such a fashion as to be nonpartisan, thereby not causing half the congregation to tune out or walk out. And it set the stage for consideration of a State of the Faith address delivered by Jesus 2,000 years ago. Notice the carefully crafted segue from introduction to exegesis.

In the fourth chapter of the book of Genesis there is a story which I believe holds the key to the problem of violence in our time. It is the story of Cain and Abel. It happens to be a story about murder. Now I think I perhaps need to get your permission to talk to you about an event in which murder was the central event. I will understand perfectly if you think, "No, no, not another story about murder." For the society in which we live is so filled with news of abuse, of children, of spouses, of the elderly. We also hear daily about drug related crimes, drive-by shootings, systemic evils which drain the lifeblood from people, until I will understand if you were thinking, "Please not another story about murder or about violence." But hold on with me for just a little while.

There are several reasons why I think I ought to be able to urge you to please give this story one more chance. In the first place I should let you know that I am not one of those nay-saying preachers, always coming up with the list of ten things that we all lament. I happen to be a more positive preacher in general. I grew up around the old Piggly Wiggly theme that says, As you go through life, my brother, what'er may be your goal, keep your eye on the donut and not on the hole. So usually, I'm very positive about what I am preaching about.

But there's another reason why I want you to hold on with me in regards to this story of murder, of intrigue between brothers. Secondly, because, you see, as I travel all over this nation, people keep asking me, "Jim, what can we do to turn the tide of murder and hate and violence?" I believe that we who are preachers and community leaders and church leaders have a responsibility to at least address the issue of violence. Though we hate to hear the name itself—murder, destruction, violation—but we have an obligation.

And really, the third reason why I want you to hear the story of Cain and Abel is because this story while its theme is the murder of Abel by his brother Cain also reveals the root of violence, where it comes from. And then with a Christian understanding, from my perspective,

I'm able to see that it also reveals to us what it is that is the source of our
hope to a world that is no longer filled with violence. So, let me turn to
this story.[3]

In that sermon introduction, Jim Forbes, widely regarded to be one of
America's greatest preachers, gives evidence of why he is so acclaimed.
Consider all he accomplishes in one simple introduction: (1) He acknowledges our general fear of violence. Especially when speaking to an urban
congregation in New York City, his opening paragraph touches the listeners where they live, giving them permission to confess a level of fear that
exists among almost all city-dwellers each time they read the morning
news. (2) He acknowledges that this is both a biblical and pertinent topic,
and that people expect some word from the pulpit to address it. (3) He
articulates a word of hope that is based on a proper understanding of
Christian faith. Thus, the people who have confessed inner fears and
accepted corporate responsibility to face said fears are also comforted with
the ultimate assurance of hope. (4) Dr. Forbes segues beautifully into his
exegesis of the text: "So let me turn to this story."

We have a word to speak to the people. It is THE Word of all words.
But, people do not listen unless speakers first grab their attention. To do
less dishonors The Word and the One who called us to proclaim it. The
front porch is the entry into the house of faith, and thus should be both
tidy and inviting.

NOTES

1. Jim Standiford, "A Triple-Espresso Faith," 13 November 2005, sermon, First
United Methodist Church, San Diego CA, http://www.fumcsd.org/mediafiles/
zsr111305pdf.pdf.

2. Stephen Huber, "Jesus' Inaugural Sermon," 31 January 2010, sermon, National
Cathedral, Washington DC, http://www.nationalcathedral.org/worship/sermonTexts/
sh20100131.shtm.

3. James A. Forbes, "If Cain Had Only Known," 1996, sermon, Riverside Church,
New York NY.

CHAPTER 2

The Formula: Exegete

Once the congregation is on board, it is the preacher's task to state the biblical case. The people did not come first and foremost seeking the clergyperson's wisdom. That is important, but it is not primary. It is divine wisdom the listeners' seek. The reason people pay attention to sermons is because they hope within those spoken messages to hear some word from God specifically for them. This is why it has always been my practice to read the Scripture lesson immediately before the sermon. It is a symbol to my people, telling them that what they are about to hear is born of the written testaments of our faith and not just some intriguing or inspiring idea from a public speaker. For that, go listen to Wayne Dyer or Deepak Chopra. They are good at what they do. But church is the place and the time to hear a word that is uniquely faith-based and consistent with the textbook of that particular faith.

In seminary, we all learned the difference between eisegesis and exegesis. It is the difference between proclaiming what I want to say and proclaiming what the Bible actually teaches. There is never a justification for writing a sermon then seeking a text to match it. Instead, we are called to allow the biblical stories to take us (and our people) where they will, even if the texts surprise us by dropping us on some shore of Nineveh.

I heard the pastor of a rather conservative congregation explain to his church that Jesus' first miracle really had nothing to do with wine. The liquid, he maintained, was not at all like our current wine. It was not fermented, just a kind of strong grape juice. Thus, he contended, Jesus was not in any way suggesting that people should ingest strong drink. Rather, the point of the miracle was to show Christ's power in providing all our needs. Interesting. Of course, it is absolutely inconsistent with the biblical narrative. First of all, those who tasted the beverage Jesus created referred to it as "wine" in the traditional sense, and even said that it had a better flavor than that which had already been consumed. This, they said, should have been served first, and then when people were under the influence of its magic (i.e., tipsy), a cheaper wine could have been served without complaint (John 2:10). In short, it was an alcoholic beverage. There is really no reasonable way to debate that. And what about the preacher's message that Jesus performed the miracle to display his power to meet all our needs? Actually, John reported the miracle for that purpose, not Jesus. In fact, it is clear that Jesus did not originally intend to perform the miracle at all and even seemed a bit irritated to have been asked. "Woman, what have you to do with me? [Why are you requesting this?] My hour has not yet come!" The story demands to tell itself. We are neither authors nor redactors; we are reporters.

Consider the tragic eisegetical statements some preachers have made across the years based on a few verses recorded in the letters to the Corinthian churches. Men (almost without fail) quote the following two verses about the role of women in church: "Let your women keep silent in the churches, for they are not permitted to speak; but they are to be submissive, as the law also says. And if they want to learn something, let them ask their own husbands at home; for it is shameful for women to speak in church." Read the words. Shut the Bible. And launch into a homiletical tirade that demeans women and misreads Paul. For eons, some preachers have done just that with those verses, justifying the oppression of women by appealing to the text's dictum that they should be "submissive," simply learning from men (i.e., their husbands). The practice of interpreting this particular text resulted in denominational refusals to ordain women into ministry as well as male-dominated households and even societies, as for centuries culture was primarily shaped by men who justified their misogyny by appealing to Scripture.

Now suppose one puts the text into context. What do we quickly learn? We learn that this verse was written specifically to the infant church in Corinth, not to the catholic Church *ad infinitum*. What Paul wrote here is neither repeated nor practiced in his other writings or ministry. In fact, frequently in other New Testament passages, either Paul or those writing about him refer to the leadership of numerous women in the early Church (even as evangelists and preachers). He discouraged that practice merely in the city of Corinth. Why? Because Corinth had practiced what Paul considered pagan religions, particularly as related to the Temple of Aphrodite. In that temple, which was a very popular religious house in Corinth for a long period of history, women navigated the ship. They were the teachers, the priestesses ("liturgists," we would say), and the persons who set the course of ministry for the congregation. Men attended, listened, learned, and obeyed. And some of the dictates of those in charge were inconsistent with what Paul considered to be appropriate moral behavior.

Paul admittedly had some intriguing ideas about human sexuality. Freud would have had a field day with the apostle. However, even had that not been the case, the Temple of Aphrodite would still have been a symbol of everything Paul feared and held in disdain. One of the common Aphrodite practices was "temple prostitution." Men would go to church and have sex with a priestess, literally as a religious ritual. This was functionally similar to the practice of animal sacrifice liturgy in ancient Judaism and early Christianity. The theory was that the man offered himself up to the goddess Aphrodite, who, pleased with the offering, would then grant him and his household fertility blessings, which could be applied to either the birth of children or plentiful agricultural crops. It was a ritualistic sowing of seed, with the faith-expectation being the blessing of a specific harvest.

When Paul wrote his advice to the infant Christian congregation in Corinth, it was his way of saying, "We are doing a new thing, so new, in fact, that everything you recall about your former religion is now turned upside down." Obviously, when one is converted from a former religious practice to a new one, the individual brings along a mental catalogue of what it means to be religious. If, for example, a group of former Lutherans decided to create the religion of Zorduk, one could safely imagine that however Zorduk was worshiped would resemble how God had been worshiped when they were still Lutherans. They would have only one set of ideas regarding what it meant to worship a deity. The same was true for those folks in Corinth. Though they might have accepted Paul's God as revealed in the Carpenter from Nazareth, their understanding of worship and corporate religion was still fashioned by their lives spent in the Temple of Aphrodite. So Paul had to make it unquestionably clear that they were now doing a new thing in a new way that disowned everything that went before. Thus, women (including ex-priestesses who had converted) were told that they could not even speak in this new church. This was not a universal law for *the* Church, just a specific principle for *that* church. If we are going to preach on that passage, we are under a divine mandate to preach it honestly and authentically—to exegete, not to eisegete. We provide a disservice to our congregation, to women, and to Paul if we fail to explain, at least in part, why those verses are not meant to be universal and that

Paul did, in fact, rely heavily on the ministry of women in other first-century communities.

It is critical to spend adequate time with the Bible for any biblically based sermon. That statement is profoundly obvious, and yet it needs to be said. It is not enough to quote a text and then flee to the green pastures of our own imagination. That is, however, too often the temptation for any gifted religious speaker. We understand the text. We have spent preparation time and prayer time with it. We sat in seminary classrooms listening to professors explain it. And by now we have numerous fascinating ideas born of it that we simply cannot wait to share with our people. But our people have not given that same time or attention to the lesson. For many of them, it is the first time they have been encountered by that text, let alone by its context. We cannot effectively apply until we have first effectively exegeted.

When preparing sermons, preachers must constantly remind ourselves: to linger is to listen. Put another way, it is hard for our congregations to hear God's voice in Scripture if we do not allow them to linger with Scripture long enough to catch the whispers. This is admittedly a fine line for the preacher. Race past a lesson or text too quickly, and you (a) almost inevitably eisegete and (b) almost inevitably give the impression that your own thoughts are the source of the morning's wisdom. On the other hand, stay with the text or lesson too long, and the congregation (a) feels that it is in a history class and (b) begins to ask the understandable question, "So what does any of this have to do with me?" How do we avoid these pitfalls?

Let me offer three simple suggestions. *First, lay claim to the narrative power of the Bible.* Both Old and New Testaments are written in forms that master storytellers envy and emulate. It is not a book of dusty old dictums—"Thou shalt not" this and "Thou shalt" that. It is, instead, a living, breathing, and very engaging collection of stories. When a biblical lesson is properly repeated and explained to an audience, it becomes virtually a mental movie. Tell the stories as they are. Portray the characters as they were. From Charlton Heston's Moses to Bill Cosby's Noah to Susan Hayward's Bathsheba, there is nothing dull about the people who populate the pages of Scripture.

You want a good action story? Then read and proclaim Joshua's story as it is written; or the tales of Gideon; of Shadrach, Meshach, and Abednigo; of Samson; or David going out to meet Goliath. You want stories with intrigue? How about Rahab or Esther? Human interest that gets a pretty steamy R-rating? Try Ruth and Boaz, Samson and Delilah, or the Syrophoenician woman at Jacob's well. The stories Jesus told virtually tell themselves. You can picture the heroes and villains and sympathetic figures in every twist and turn. The Good Samaritan. The Prodigal Son. The Widow's Mite. There are countless characters whose opinions hold mirrors to our own, forcing us to see sides of ourselves that we prefer to deny, like watching ourselves on a movie screen: the elder brother; the rich, young ruler; Paul, the preacher of grace, refusing grace to John Mark and losing his friend Barnabas in the process.

Even passages that we do not necessarily identify as "narrative" possess those qualities when the text is set in proper context. Tell the story of why Paul wrote what he wrote about women to the people of Corinth, and your listeners' ears will perk up! In the "birth narratives," don't just read the words of an angel spoken to Mary. Explain what their impact would have been on the emotions of a teenaged, unwed girl in that age and culture. Don't just read the dream whispers of an angel to Joseph. Explain what "betrothed" meant, and the leap of faith he was asked to take, and the shame that leap could have brought not only upon Mary, but upon Joseph as well. Then go a bit further and share why, in one Gospel, the angel speaks to Mary, but in the other the angel speaks to Joseph. It is the same message with the same instruction (about the naming of the child). Why is it told differently?

Consider a passage which, on the surface, appears about as slow-moving and uninspiring as any in Matthew's telling of the birth story: the genealogy in chapter 1 ("and Solomon the father of Rehoboam, and Rehoboam the father of Abijah, and Abijah the father of Asaph, and Asaph the father of Jehoshaphat," [Matt 1:7-8] etc., yawn, etc.). That genealogy goes on for forty-two generations! (A word of advice should you pick that passage: do not read the total pericope. Just pick a few verses that get the point across and connect the important dots, and let the congregation assume the rest.) What could be less inspiring than the genealogy in the first chapter of Matthew? But what if you confess that as you exegete it? What if you go one step further and ask,

Why is that even in there? Why would those people who first read it care any more than you and I do? [*Then you tell them.*] I used to skip those verses, to be honest.

In fact, to be really honest, sometimes I still do. However, I did some investigating and learned that they really are a bit more important than I first imagined.

You tell them that Matthew was written primarily to a Hebrew audience. And to a Hebrew in that day and age, the first question in authenticating a messianic claim was not "What miracles did he do?" Heal the sick. Walk on water. Raise the dead. None of that seals the deal unless Jesus was also directly linked to Abraham and David. Otherwise, he was just another pretender to the messianic title. So Matthew did his homework and traced Jesus' family tree all the way back to those two patriarchs. You are exegeting a passage by telling them a story. So you continue:

> The genealogy ends with "Jacob, the father of Joseph, the husband of Mary, of whom Jesus was born, who is called Christ" (Mt 1:16). And far from being boring, that is suddenly our "Ah ha!" moment. That's why the genealogy matters. And that's why it would not have bored a Hebrew audience at all, but would instead have inspired them. It linked Jesus to David and Abraham, and thus in the minds of those readers, Jesus could logically be the messiah.

By this point, obviously, someone in the congregation who is thinking ahead of you is already saying, "That's a moot point because Joseph wasn't Jesus' biological dad. Who cares who Joseph was related to?" Give voice to that. Pause at this point in the exegesis and state it.

> I know some of you out there are asking, What difference does it make who Joseph was related to? Wasn't Mary supposed to have been a virgin? And didn't the angel tell that frightened little teenaged girl that she would conceive "of the Holy Spirit" (Lk 1:35)? So after all those forty-two generations of connecting Jesus back to David and Abraham, what difference does it make? It all happened through Joseph. And Joseph isn't the real father.

Then you get to expose them to a bit of historical knowledge: that in Jewish thought and custom in that age, whichever male relative named a child was at that moment considered "father." The biology of conception took a back seat to the predisposition of culture. Give the child a name, and you are the child's father. And that is why it was so important in Matthew's Gospel (unlike Luke) for Joseph, not Mary, to name the baby.

Once he had done that, he was deemed the father of the child, and suddenly his genealogy connected Jesus to David and Abraham.

Claim the narrative nature of Scripture. Unfold particular stories in such a fashion that people tune in and thus hear *the* story. Hebrew Scripture and the New Testament are filled with mental movies.

Second, illustrate the Bible's message where needed. As you tell a biblical story, periodically feel free to clarify what it says using images your audience can relate to. Jesus did that all the time. For example, when he told the story of the Good Samaritan, it was to illustrate in contemporary images his reference to certain verses from the Torah. It was his way of saying, "Let me share with you what this means in our lives." Then he used a form of rabbinical teaching called *midrash* (more or less a story that explains the Greater Story). "A certain man went down from Jerusalem to Jericho, and fell among thieves . . ." and off he went, weaving an illustration that captured the essence of the text he was teaching. He described a road with which they were all familiar, a winding descent lined with boulders where robbers hid and often preyed upon individuals who were traveling alone. He described the fear that people feel when we stumble upon a stranger in need. He likewise described the sense of inconvenience that is so common when we have a destination, a plan, and a deadline, and the needs of someone else get in the way. He even used familiar characters in surprising ways. His story was engaging and real and captured the attention of the listeners in such a fashion that it made his treatment of an old text unmistakably clear. If Jesus did that in his preaching, why shouldn't we?

In exegeting the genealogy passage from the first chapter of Matthew, for example, when addressing the importance of Joseph's naming the baby, I might pause and illustrate,

> When I read this part of the passage, it's more than just a Scripture lesson. Though having no idea what it feels like to be messianic, I do know what it feels like to be given a name and thus be made part of a family. I was adopted when I was seven weeks old. I was taken from a foster home and welcomed into another home by two lovely and loving people whose last name was Brown. They gave me their name, and thus connected me to their family. Suddenly, "Baby number 7," or whatever I was called before, became "Michael Brown." I had a name. And because of the ones who gave it to me, I had a family and a heritage: grandparents and aunts and uncles and cousins and a history going back from generation

to generation for hundreds of years down in North Carolina. I was given their name, and I became their child. Joseph gave the baby a name, and he was forever after Joseph's child—linked back generation to generation all the way to David and Abraham.

Hopefully, that brief illustration helps the congregation ponder and personalize the text. It is appropriate and often helpful to illustrate a text while exegeting it, thereby maintaining clarity of understanding in the minds of the listeners.

Third, feel free to weave the application part of the sermon into the exegesis part of the sermon. The upcoming chapter will be devoted to applying the text to the lives of the hearers. However, to flash forward only momentarily, there is an overlap that needs to be mentioned. At times, the exegesis and the application are inextricably woven together.

Suppose, for example, one is preaching a sermon constructed upon the story of the elder brother from Luke 15. While exegeting the passage, it makes sense along the way to pause and apply. Quote a text from the story: "All these years I have served you, but you never gave me a calf to make merry with my friends."

You know, for those of us who were ever children whose parents assigned us chores, something within us resonates with the elder brother's words. We probably know about being obedient, but doing so begrudgingly. I grew up in a home with no dishwasher. So following dinner, my mom expected me to help. She would wash, while I rinsed and dried. Or vice versa. I frequently thought, "Why should I have to do this? What am I getting out of it? Not so much as a nickel! It's just not fair." Children think that way, even grown-up children like the older brother in this parable. [Quote the following text: "Son, all that I have is yours."] That was quite literally true. The younger brother had already received his inheritance. There is no reason to believe he would receive more. All that remained would someday belong to the older brother. He just didn't see it at the time, much as I didn't think things through when I was washing plates after dinner. Somehow it didn't occur to me that dad had paid for the groceries and mom had shopped for them. She had also cooked the food and put it on the table, as she would do again the next night and the next. All I had to do was show up and eat . . . and then wash place-settings for three people. Sometimes (as Paul put it), when we think like a child, we miss the big picture.

It is often helpful in the midst of the exegetical stage of the sermon to provide brief illustrations that connect *the* story to *our* story. It does not take the place of the greater (be that general or more specific) application component of the message that is yet to come. It simply helps the listener more clearly identify with the passage being considered.

This may be especially helpful when the passage is not one written in a traditional narrative form. In truth, the parables tell themselves. Their messages are abundantly clear. It is rarely necessary to help the listener access their central ideas. However, suppose your passage comes from one of the pastoral epistles, or perhaps one of the legal dictums from Leviticus or Deuteronomy. In those cases, it is wise for the preacher periodically (and briefly) to pause during the exegesis in order to help clarify what the passage actually means. And that is superbly done by use of illustrative material. I once heard a minister exegeting the Ten Commandments, and I've paraphrased the passage about coveting a neighbor's donkey.

> I remember doing that once. My neighbor had a black Jaguar. It was the prettiest car I had ever seen. "Covet" is barely adequate to describe how much I yearned for that car, or how much I resented him for owning it. I finally made him an offer he couldn't refuse, and he sold it to me. One month later I had to have the engine repaired. It cost more than the list price of many cars. Two months later, the transmission went out. That's when I began to understand how wise this particular Commandment is.

To be sure, his words were rather folksy and homespun. However, they went directly to the heart of the word "covet" (meaning not merely to desire that which belongs to someone else, but also to resent the other person for possessing it). In all likelihood, the congregation thereafter remembered that meaning because of that illustration. On another occasion, I heard a minister quote the text, "And the wise men returned to their home by another way." He paused, then said to his congregation:

> I know the feeling. In the third grade, I left the school building every afternoon through a different door so that Jeffrey, the bully, couldn't find me. The Wise Men were doing the same thing so that Herod, the bully, couldn't find them, and more especially, so that he couldn't find Jesus.

Just that quickly, a text that seemed like little more than a relatively inconsequential travel detail became alive, familiar, and pertinent.

Sample Sermon Exegeses

Though preached over sixty years ago, Dietrich Bonhoeffer's telling of the Gideon story is fresh in his approach to exegeting the passage and connecting it with his audience. Consider how he related that Old Testament story so that it powerfully intersected with the contemporary story of his listeners in World War II Germany. Bonhoeffer and his audience were witnessing the cruelties of Naziism, modern-day Midianites. Someone needed to "deliver oppressed Israel out of the hand of overpowering enemies." People of faith heard the call to stand up and speak out but were understandably intimidated. Eventually, however, as Martin Niemoller would later point out, if we witness injustice and remain too long silent, when the enemy comes for us, there is no one left to speak out. All that emerges from Bonhoeffer's brilliant exegesis of an Old Testament passage about Gideon.

> Here is Gideon, one among thousands; but out of these thousands, God encounters him and calls him into service, calls him into action. Why indeed him; why indeed you and me? Can God not call whom he wants, high or low, weak or strong, poor or rich, without our beginning to argue? Is there any possibility other than to hear and obey?
>
> Gideon is supposed to deliver oppressed Israel out of the hand of their overpowering enemies, the Midianites. He, who is like a thousand others, is called to do something no one has done before. He looks upon himself and his strength, and he looks upon the unbeatably strong opposition. He has nothing in his hand; the enemy has everything. And he spoke to God: "Lord, whereby shall I save Israel? How shall I accomplish that for which you have called me? Lord, your commission is too great. Don't be cruel. Take it away from me. Or else let me see help—give me armies, weapons, riches—God, you don't know how we are suffering. Look at the starving, fainting people; look how they despair of you, without home, without bread . . . ." We know this Gideon, don't we! He takes a face we recognize. Gideon, we know your voice only too well; you speak today just like you did then.[1]

Consider how Barbara Brown Taylor illustrates her exegesis of Jesus' self-description as "the good shepherd." It is all part of making the ancient text clear by employing contemporary or familiar imagery.

> "I am the good shepherd. The good shepherd lays down his life for the sheep." That is what makes him good, according to John—his willingness to get involved, to risk his life for the life of his flock. *His* flock. Not somebody else's flock, which he gets paid five dollars an hour to look after, but his own flock—the one he has bought and bred, doctored and protected. He is invested in it, in more ways than one.
>
> His sheep are his livelihood, for one thing, but they are also his extended family. They know his voice, his touch, his walk. If they are grazing with a thousand other sheep and he calls them, they will separate themselves from the crowd and follow him home. His flute is the sound of safety for them—the sound of still waters and green pastures. He knows them too, by name and disposition: Houdini, who is always escaping through some hole in the fence; Pegleg, who limps from the time she stepped in a hole; Bossy, who likes nothing better than butting heads.
>
> There is something about ownership that creates intimacy, especially ownership of living things. A dog or a cat can become a soul friend who knows how you are feeling when no one else does. I have a cat named Merlin who is my spiritual director. When I am frantic, he goes to sleep on my lap. When I am sad, he leaps out at me from dark corners, and when I am fine he takes a break and goes off to do his own thing. Some people say we pick pets who look like us. If it is true, it is because they really are extensions of us, creatures who are so much a part of our lives that sometimes it is not easy to tell who owns whom.[2]

Having read that, who can ever again read John 10:11 without a deeper sense of the passion the Good Shepherd feels for us?

Our source of faith is the Bible. And remember, we are not so much redactors as reporters. The text must say what the text is designed to say. People listen to our sermons hoping that our messages are rooted in an ancient faith and literary corpus of wisdom that contains a message that can make sense of their lives. We do our listeners justice by doing the texts justice—explaining those texts accurately, in context, in an interesting and clear way, and then allowing the texts to take the congregation where *they* will (sometimes as opposed to where *we* would). The second part of the formula for effective preaching is always effective exegesis.

NOTES

1. Dietrich Bonhoeffer, "Gideon," in *Twenty Centuries of Great Preaching*, vol. 20. (Waco TX: Word Books, 1971) 128–29.

2. Barbara Brown Taylor, "The Shepherd's Flute," in *Bread of Angels* (Cambridge MA: Cowley Publications, 1997) 81.

CHAPTER 3

The Formula: Apply

At some point it all boils down to a single question that each listener will pose in his or her mind: "So what?" Occasionally in a sermon I will give voice to that question for my listeners. "All right, by this time I know what you're thinking: 'What does this have to do with me, my life, my family, my world?'" Whether or not you acknowledge the questions, they are there.

It is a fine balance that must be maintained by any preacher, the balance between textual integrity and contextual relevance. Always the temptation exists to simply tell the biblical story, assuming your listeners will draw their own conclusions. And, to be sure, there is something to be said for such expository efforts. *The* story speaks to *our* stories in individual and unique ways. Perhaps it is our call simply to allow that to happen. Still, if one does nothing but report and exegete, he or she has simply delivered a lecture. Teaching a lesson is appropriate in the seminary or in a Sunday school class but not to the same degree in the pulpit. The discipline of preaching includes the act of teaching but is not limited to it.

By the same token, the temptation exists to be prophetic or pastoral to such a degree that textual matters are virtually irrelevant. At some point, all of us who preach professionally have been tempted (and probably have yielded) to write a sermon on a topic we wished to address, afterward seeking diligently to find a text that was consistent with what we had already composed. Admittedly, maybe our thoughts were inspired. Maybe they were timely. Maybe they were helpful. But they were not examples of authentic preaching, because preaching in the Christian tradition issues forth from the scriptural lesson. The lesson is never a mere limb grafted onto the tree of the preacher's pet topic. There are moments when the occasion sets the theme: Homecoming, Stewardship Sunday, Easter, Pentecost, etc. There are moments when certain themes demand our attention. What preacher on the Sunday following 9/11 would have chosen to ignore that topic from the pulpit? But whatever sets the theme of the day, it is the biblical story that frames and expresses that theme for the people.

Again, on the Sunday following 9/11, when churches all across America had standing-room-only crowds, those worshipers did not come asking, "What does the minister think about all this?" They came "with groans too great for words" (Rom 8:26), desperate to know, "How does our faith respond to all this?"

There truly is a fine balance that must be maintained between the text of the sermon and the context of the preacher's and listeners' world. It is required that the preacher live in both worlds, much as Karl Barth suggested when he said a preacher should enter the pulpit equipped with a Bible in one hand and a newspaper in the other.

In our world, for example, how can one not address the concern of environmentalism? The overwhelming majority of the world's most respected scientists concur that global warming is an undeniable reality, that polar icecaps are melting, that significant inhabitable land masses could shrink into the sea, and that our time to take corrective action is limited. It is unimaginable that persons who possess both public voice and influence would choose to fiddle while that particular Rome burns.

The Torah begins with the divine mandate that we carefully tend to God's creation. To be given "dominion" over planet earth quite literally means "stewardship." God calls (commands, expects) God's people to take care of this one earth which is ours. Stewardship of the planet is not an option, either theologically or practically. Even those who do not believe in global warming can still agree that ecological responsibility is a divine calling. From simple littering to the endangered-species list, everyone, regardless of politics or posture on science, understands that God has entrusted the earth to us, and we have not done a good job of protecting it. It is an act of faithful discipleship to be environmentally conscious and active.

Whether or not we know what to say on the topic, our congregants will demand that we say something about theodicy. We preach to people who bring pains and fears to church by the boatload. And at some deep point they ask the Kushner question, wondering how a loving God can permit such bad things to happen to basically good people?

Sunday by Sunday I look out at the same faces that every other preacher sees in her or his congregation. There is a woman struggling with cancer, hoping against hope that perhaps this round of chemo will be more effective than the others were. There is a man whose job was downsized, and he's in his late fifties and is no longer particularly marketable. Seated alongside him is his wife, with an understandably worn and worried countenance. Beside her sits two children, a son in his junior year at college and a daughter in her senior year of high school. And those parents have no idea how to come up with one semester's tuition for either child. There is a woman whose husband walked out after twenty years. There was no warning. She didn't see it coming. She feels abandoned and alone. There is a man who trusted his partner but was recently diagnosed with an illness that his partner passed along to him from somebody else. So now he deals not only with compromised health but also with shattered trust. There is a woman who waits tables and barely manages to get by, and with every failed casting call she watches her dream of being a performer grow dimmer. There are the faces of people struggling with the inevitable concerns of aging, whether those issues are guilt, grief, a sense of failure, memory problems, loneliness, financial difficulties, or a fear of their own mortality. There are the faces of people who have stood at gravesites saying good-byes they were not prepared to say, and their broken hearts have never entirely healed. The list is endless. The point is simply that in every place where two or three are gathered together, there in the midst of them are sorrow and sadness, failure and fear, heartache and heartbreak. And they harbor the hope that this spokesperson of faith who stands before them will have something of value to say, something that either helps heal the hurt or at least gives them the strength to endure it. From the days of Job until our own days, there has been no clear and definitive answer to the question of why people suffer. But from those days till ours, the theodicy question persists, and preachers cannot ignore it, nor can we ignore the pain of those who ask.

In our world, how can one avoid dealing with the topic of intolerance? When one reads of young persons who are bullied or commit harassment-induced suicide, or women, children, or the aged who are abused, or racial conflicts and prejudice, how can one in good conscience turn away? A simple reading of the New Testament precludes doing so. "This is my commandment," said Jesus, "that you love one another" (John 13:34). "You shall love your neighbor as yourself" (Matt 22:39). "In as much as you have refused kindness to one of the least of these, who are my brothers and sisters, you have done so likewise unto me" (Matt 25:45). "You cannot love God, whom you have not seen, and hate your brother or sister, whom you have seen" (1 John 4:20). Biblical preachers are not allowed the privilege of ignoring the topic of intolerance. Or expand the topic and call it injustice. When you are made aware of the genocide in Darfur, how can you justify giving your people a steady diet of nothing more than "Helpful Hints for Being Happy"?

Psychologists tell us that the most debilitating of all human emotions is guilt. If that is so, then clergy are in a unique position to provide a healing balm. We call it "grace," and it is the centerpiece of all Christian teaching. As Paul advised, "Where sin increased, grace increased all the more" (Rom 5:20). The loving naiveté of Rauschenbusch truly has long-since passed, nor in this world can any believe that "every day in every way, we are getting better and better."[1] However, the doctrine of grace assures God's love for us not "because of" but, indeed, "in spite of."

After more than thirty-six years in ordained ministry, I have certainly lost count of the number of persons who have confessed to me that they never felt loved, which they believed was the source of whatever dysfunction they brought to my office. Hundreds reported growing up in homes where love was neither displayed nor expressed, where discipline was severe, and where they were made to feel responsible for that environment of unhappiness. Likewise, numerous persons have shared with me the memory of being reared in churches where guilt was not reduced but was instead induced. Do most individuals have reasons for feeling guilty? Of course we do. We have missed the mark (*hamartia*) more often than we wish to remember, but the memories persist and the memories haunt us. We are aware of that. But we in ministry possess a greater awareness, which is that God's love for us is unconditional. We have a sacred opportunity to speak that truth to those who are burdened by guilt that has been heaped upon them from family, institutional religion, and memory. We have the chance to bring healing that restores life. In a world where guilt (whether real or imagined) robs individuals of "life abundant" (John 10:10), we have the chance to give it back. We who preach cannot refuse to champion grace.

One cannot serve as pastor of a church for more than an hour without recognizing the inevitable presence of personal pain, which is inherent whenever "two or three are gathered together" (Matt 18:20).

When I was just beginning in ministry, I heard a lecture by the late Dr. John Sutherland Bonnell (for many years the revered senior minister of Fifth Avenue Presbyterian Church in New York City). In it, he told the story of shaking hands in the narthex of his church following a worship service. As he greeted people, he noticed a woman lingering nearby.

Though he did not recognize the woman, he did recognize her desire to speak with him. After shaking the last hand, Dr. Bonnell walked to her and asked how he could be of help.

"I'm sure you don't remember me," she began. "I was here three years ago, only once. My daughter was in the Manhattan Eye, Ear, and Nose Hospital. They had discovered a tumor behind her left eye. In order to save her life, the surgeons had to remove the eye in order to remove the growth. I came here the Sunday before her surgery in order to pray for the strength for our family to get through that. Well, we got through it. She went home and did fine for three years. But now she is back with a tumor behind her right eye." At that point the woman paused to collect herself emotionally. After a long moment, she continued.

"Tomorrow they will remove her right eye. So I know that after tonight, she will never see my face again. She will never see her father's face or her brother's. She will never see her little dog, whom she loves so much, or the green of grass, or the blue of sky. If she goes to her prom, she will never see the dress she wears. If she gets married, she will never look into her husband's face or those of her children." Again, the distraught mother paused as her emotions overcame her.

At last she looked back at Dr. Bonnell and made the statement, "I came here today hoping to find the strength to face tomorrow."

Dr. Bonnell said in his lecture,

Suddenly I found myself thinking, "What in God's name did I say today to help that mother find what she needed most of all?" It became a fulcrum moment in my life as a preacher. I decided that day that every Sunday, someone may be in a pew who has come to church as their last stop in the search for hope. And I would not enter the pulpit without a word of hope every Sunday, a word to help some other struggler find the strength to face tomorrow![2]

People come into our churches desperate and frightened, burdened by personal pains. That is the world our congregations live in. And whereas they need sound theology and proper exegesis, down deep in their hearts they also need to know how it helps them carry the weights and loads of their lives.

By this point, I suspect each reader is imagining a personal litany of topics, a list of issues which pervade life on this planet and thus frame our experience of all things, including faith. Anger, grief, materialism, patriotism, hope, despair, loneliness, finding a sense of purpose, human sexuality, ecumenism, war, fear, happiness, etc. . . . the list is long and pertinent. That is the key word: *pertinent.* These are the avenues we journey or fear or seek day by day in life. And if the faith proclaimed does not intersect hearers on those avenues, then it simply does not pertain. It is not pertinent or relevant. And we commit the travesty of hiding the Light of the World under a bushel (Matt 5:15). We are called to apply God's truth to the lives of our listeners who attend church, ultimately, in search of that truth and what it might mean for them.

Sample Sermon Applications

In his sermon "Message in the Stars," Frederick Beuchner reflects on biblical mandates: "Be brave . . . be merciful . . . feed my lambs . . . press on toward the goal." How do we respond to those commands? When do the center-stage moments come when we are to perform our faith with faithfulness? Perhaps the moment when faith is put to the test is not so much center stage as subtle.

> A face comes toward us down the street. Do we raise our eyes or do we keep them lowered, passing by in silence? Somebody says something about somebody else, and what he says happens to be not only cruel but also funny, and everybody laughs. Do we laugh too, or do we speak the truth? When a friend has hurt us, do we take pleasure in hating him, because hate has its pleasures as well as love, or do we try to build back some flimsy little bridge? Sometimes when we are alone, thoughts come swarming into our heads like bees—some of them destructive, ugly, self-defeating thoughts, some of them creative and glad. Which thoughts do we choose to think then, as much as we have the choice? Will we be brave today or a coward today? Not in some big way but probably in some little foolish way, yet brave still. Will we be honest today or a liar? Just some little pint-sized honesty, but honest still. Will we be a friend or cold as ice today?[3]

In a sermon titled "How to Deal with Loneliness," Robert McCracken explored with his congregation at Riverside Church the parable of the Prodigal Son. He conjectured that one reason the son returned to his father's house was out of a sense of loneliness for home, for community, for love. But the return was a decision he alone could make. No one else, even those who stood prepared to welcome him, could make the decision for him. A decision we, too, can make—an action we can take—when caught in the throes of loneliness is to consciously reach out to others. McCracken commended that biblical principle to his congregation.

> So I say, Get out of yourself and into the lives of others. Be friendly if you would have friends. You know that you never forget the hand that was reached out to you in your hour of loneliness and despair. It is the people who live unto themselves who are generally left to themselves. Somebody has said, "Until I loved, I was alone." So speak a cheerful word to your neighbor. Offer a helping hand to those who are in difficulties. Sympathize when people are up against it and fighting a hard battle.[4]

The application was clear and concise. The prescription for battling loneliness, based on a biblical principle from the Gospel of Luke, was simply to have a friend, be a friend.

How powerfully Martin Luther King, Jr., applied the text after carefully exegeting the passage from Daniel where Nebudchadnezzar's government asked the people to bow down and worship a golden idol, but Shadrach, Meshach, and Abednigo refused to bow. Dr. King simply remarked (and it became a galvanizing, rallying cry to action):

> There comes a time when moral humans can't obey a law which their conscience tells them is unjust. And I tell you this morning, my friends, that history has moved on, and great moments have often come forth, because there were those individuals in every age and every generation who were willing to say, "I will be obedient to a higher law."[5]

There is a moment during every sermon you preach when the listener will inevitably ask, "So what? What does this have to do with me, my life, my world?" That is the moment when you are able to build a bridge from the days of Scripture to the present day. The bridge is essential. Whether the desired result is a call to action or a gift of comfort, sermons are intended to do more than merely provide information about biblical texts. Engage. Exegete. And then *apply*.

NOTES

1. Emile Coue, *Self-Mastery through Conscious Autosuggestion* (http://www.gutenberg.org/ebooks/27203).

2. From a recording of Bonnell's address to the Manhasset Conference for Clergy, c. 1950s. Housed at Reigner Library, Union Theological Seminary, Richmond VA.

3. Frederick Beuchner, *The Magnificent Defeat* (New York: Seabury Press, 1979) 48–49.

4. Robert McCracken, "How to Deal with Loneliness," *The Riverside Preachers*, ed. Paul H. Sherry (New York: Pilgrim Press, 1978) 78.

5. Rev. Dr. Martin Luther King Jr., "But If Not," 5 November 1967, Ebeneezer Baptist Church, Atlanta GA (https://www.youtube.com/watch?v=pOjpaIO2seY).

CHAPTER 4

An Exercise: Putting the Principles to Practice

There comes a time to "either step up or step back."[1] In other words, all the thoughtful consideration or careful theorizing about homiletics in which one may indulge does not a sermon make. Reading examples from other persons or advice from some guy in New York may be helpful, but you can't carry that into the pulpit. The time has come to pray, write, edit, and proclaim.

I am convinced that the formula for preaching I have been articulating in this book can be appropriated by a wide variety of speakers, not just by ordained clergy. How many times, for example, have you heard a university chancellor stand to address a graduating class? What is the speaker's usual (and usually effective) methodology? Ordinarily, there is some light word to parents (frequently about breathing a sigh of relief that tuition payments are now a thing of the past) and to graduating students (typically about no more cafeteria food or sharing dorm showers, etc.). That is the moment of *engagement*. It catches the audience's attention. Then the chancellor proceeds to remark about what the university hopes the students will take away from their four (or more) years on campus: the academic information, the hunger for increased knowledge, the wisdom that means more than data, a broader world view, the pride and loyalty inherent in being part of that particular historic institution, etc. That is a secular equivalent to *exegesis*. It is the university's way of defining the moment by placing it in its proper context. And usually, the chancellor, prior to awarding diplomas, will conclude his or her remarks by challenging students to reach high in life, to set lofty and ethical goals, and to use what they have learned on campus to build a better life in the world beyond the campus.

Or how often at some civic meeting have you heard a similar model employed? The politician or event organizer or activist will engage the crowd by using (a) humor, (b) praise with regard to the audience's obvious devotion to the issue of merit, or (c) a dramatic story that frames the issue about to be addressed. *Engagement.* The speaker then proceeds to speak about the urgency of the issue at hand and what has led to this particular moment. Pertinent information is shared, explaining the details of the issue to the persons attending. *Exegesis.* The speech is concluded with a call to action. Make a donation. Vote for our candidate. Storm city hall. Send volunteers to the site of the crisis. *Application.*

One particularly obvious and effective example of how this formula works beyond the pulpit can be seen every time PBS does its semiannual fundraising marathons. During those seasons, we are treated to wonderful musical concerts from opera to American folk, from doo-wop to "Celtic Woman." But also popular during those seasons are the self-help, motivational programs promoted by Ed Stott, Wayne Dyer, Suze Orman, and others. The speaker greets the audience with an immediate acknowledgement of why they are there: "Get rich!" "Get smart!" "Get happy!" "Get well!" *Engagement.* Then comes the presentation advising the viewers why the particular goal of the program is pertinent and what steps must be followed in order to achieve it. *Exegesis.* Finally comes what is known as "the pitch." That is the cut-away to a studio with attractive persons who are half broadcasters and half salespersons. They stand in front of numerous individuals staffing phones, each one appearing busy, taking calls from those who are obviously wise enough to know a good bargain when they see one (a visual part of the pitch). The viewer is promised a complete DVD of the evening's presentation plus other books, tapes, or DVDs that they have not yet seen if they will do what? Donate at a particular level! *Application.*

Repeat: I am convinced that the formula for preaching I have been articulating in this book can be appropriated by a wide variety of speakers, not just by ordained clergy. If you make presentations outside of church or religious settings, there is a formula here that you can still employ with only minimal modifications. If you are a teacher or a speaker within traditional religious education programming in a church (Sunday school, Bible study group, issue-oriented small group, etc.), this formula works equally as well as it does for clergy employing it in the pulpit. If an audience is not engaged, then no matter how significant your topic, it will be wasted on them. If the audience is not fed with the authentic information fundamental to the text or topic, your audience will be cheated. And if you do not help them apply the information to their daily lives in the world, your audience will have attended an entertaining and informative lecture that actually has no real lasting impact. To be "complete" from a homiletical perspective, every presentation must include *engagement, exegesis,* and *application.*

Now let's return to the beginning of this chapter, where I noted there comes a time to step up or step back. As a popular self-help guru often says, "Having set a direction, begin today."[2] We are now at that point in this chapter. I am going to provide some basic, skeletal suggestions, and you can decide whether to do these exercises or to put the book back on the shelf and go take a nap. Hopefully, you will do the former (practice the principles). Let me provide two biblical texts and one life issue. Your challenge is to put together three messages (sermons, Sunday school lessons, etc.), one on each of the topics suggested. I will offer very brief—and hopefully helpful—hints, more or less "starter kit" ideas, to assist in getting your creative process rolling. You may choose to use those suggestions or discard them. This is *your* exercise, and it must be *your* message. Let the text or the issue draw you where it will in your own unique context of ministry and life.

Message #1: Read 1 Samuel, chapter 17. Determine what parts of the pericope should be read in the service of worship or the teaching event. Preach from the portion you select.

Hints: Have you witnessed examples of individuals seeking to "wear someone else's armor," or have you ever done so yourself? Are there identifiable imposing or frightening "giants" that frighten your parishioners? Are there small solutions to great problems, like little stones in a child's slingshot? What are you going to do with the obvious element of violence that appears in this story, given our allegiance to a "Prince of Peace" (Isa 9:6)?

Message #2: Read John 11:1-43. Determine what parts of the pericope will be read in the worship service or the teaching event. Preach from the portion you select.

Hints: What do you make of Martha's and Mary's reactions to Jesus? Is there a pertinent correlation to or departure from their responses to him when he was previously a dinner guest in their home? Why did Jesus wait so long to respond to news about Lazarus's illness? Why does John indicate Jesus performed this miracle, and what does that say to us about the role of New Testament miracle stories in the life of faith? There are people in your group who have lost loved ones who were not resuscitated or perhaps who are living with a terminal illness. Can you relate this passage to them in a helpful (pastoral) way?

Message #3: Read section A of your daily newspaper. Choose a story that is receiving significant attention. (As I write this, we are inundated with stories about falling dictatorships in the Middle East, about child sexual-abuse scandals on university campuses, and about all the "occupy" movements born from the Occupy Wall Street crusade; when you read this, who knows what other hot topics will be dominating the headlines.) Find a biblical passage that speaks to you or in some way reminds you of the issue at hand. Preach from the text and relate it to the news. Do not preach from the news, attaching a text to it.

Hints: Why was this a lead story in the paper? Why and how does it connect with the listeners in your parish? If it does not, then why have you chosen to speak about it? Why did this remind you of the biblical lesson you read? What does the lesson say to your audience that can help them interpret the issue (as opposed to your interpreting the issue for them)? If it is an issue that is alarming or discouraging, can you address it with the seriousness it deserves while still providing respites—breathing places—within the manuscript, moments for your listeners to relax and reflect? Why do you think this deserves sermonic attention?

NOTES

1. Gordon Lightfoot, "Baby, Step Back," Warner Brothers/Reprise Records, 1982.

2. Jonathan Lockwood Huie, *Life Sayings* (tarunbisht.blogspot/Lockwood).

CHAPTER 5

Style

Remember a moving or effective sermon or speech you heard at some point in the past. Recall what touched you about it, what engaged your senses, and what energized your spirit as a listener. Was it simply the topic being addressed, or was it also (perhaps even more so) the manner in which the topic was shared? Now do the same in reverse fashion. Remember a moment when you went to hear a speaker with great expectations but came away feeling disappointed. Was it merely a mishandling of the material that left you dissatisfied, or did it have to do at least in part with the way the material was presented? Whereas style can never compensate for lack of substance or exist on the same level, neither can it be summarily dismissed as show and gimmick, smoke and mirrors. Style is a vehicle by which substance is transported. It can become a powerful aid in communicating truth, but by the same token can be a genuine impediment if not taken seriously. Consider two examples:

Example 1: Some years ago I was at a dinner in Washington, DC, where a sitting president of the United States was the featured speaker. The banquet hall was filled with several hundred people representing governmental, business, scientific, and faith communities. The president was an artist at winning the crowd. His appeal was obvious, and his performance was flawless. He used humor, anecdotes, philosophy, faith, and personal zeal to whip the audience into an almost revivalistic frenzy. Members of both parties (including a man soon to be his opponent in an upcoming election) were on their feet, cheering. At the close of the event, I tried to interpret what he had done and why it had been so enthusiastically received. His material was by no means deep or cerebral. It was simply a prelude to the presentation of the Congressional Medal of Honor to a beloved man who was there to be recognized. What the president said was, in fact, predictable. But it was the way he had said it that gave life to the event. It was his style that held the day.

Example 2: At another event, a man of impressive personal history told a powerful story about an incident early in his life. The incident became formative for him, guiding him in the direction of a life of singular service to at-risk youth. In written form, it was the sort of story *Guideposts* or *Chicken Soup for the Soul* would have clamored to print. However, during his presentation of the story (which was part of his personal biography), the audience saw nothing but the top of his head. He read it word for word without ever looking up, without ever once making eye contact, and without ever giving the impression that he was even remotely involved in what was being reported. And the response to his presentation did not even rise to a lukewarm level, whereas, had it been shared in a personal, conversational way, it had the potential to touch the audience in a profoundly moving fashion. He had substance, but his vehicle failed to adequately transport it.

As those who proclaim biblical and theological truth, we have been provided with substance. Our topics are the divine, the eternal, the historic, the visionary, the omnipotent and omnipresent, and how all this intersects with our daily lives (whether personal or corporate) in the contemporary world. Let me reiterate: we have been provided with substance. It is the transformative story that humankind needs to hear and consider. But, as Paul put it, "How shall they hear without a preacher?" (Rom 10:14). It is our task to present the story in such a fashion that people will, in fact, be drawn to it. That being the case, consider a few pieces of practical advice regarding the too-often dismissed matter of style.

Do Your Homework

Years ago I heard a statement made by the late Dr. John Carlton, and it has stuck with me ever since. Carlton was a distinguished professor of preaching. He was also a brilliant practitioner of the art. He said, "On Sundays when I walk out of the pulpit, the congregation may be able to say, 'I do not agree with the intent of his message.' That is fine. But, whether they agree with me or not, they should all at least be able to say, 'It is obvious that John did his homework!'"

What is our "homework"?

As has already been stated, we are expected to engage, to exegete, and to apply. None of that needs to be repeated. But in terms of style and delivery, as well as the quality of the message being prepared, there is additional homework to be done.

The words that impress themselves on the minds of serious preachers are *time* and *effort*. Sermons do not magically write themselves. Neither is it ordinarily reasonable to think that a person can research, exegete, write, review, edit, rewrite, and learn a sermon of significant quality if you get started on Saturday. The calling to share "the unsearchable riches" (Eph 3:8) demands more of us than a cavalier approach to preparation. We cheat the message and the listeners when we try to economize on time as preachers.

A friend of mine who is a gifted and scholarly preacher literally hangs a sign on his study door Monday through Thursday of every week. From 8:30 until 11:30 a.m. each morning, the sign is there. It simply says: *If someone just died, please knock.* His church people both understand and appreciate the meaning of the posted notice. He is in preparation to answer his highest calling, and that uninterrupted preparation is the greatest gift he gives to his congregation. To be sure, one by one with individuals, his greatest gifts may be love, listening skills, encouragement, mentoring, etc. But when it comes to the corporate community of faith, he understands that no mission and no meeting should supplant the sacred responsibility he bears to tell the "old, old story" in a way that touches and transforms lives.

Strong preaching begins with a kind of *lectio divina* approach to the lesson(s) to be explored in the pulpit. We read, contemplate, then read again, finding insights missed the first time through. After spending adequate personal time with the lesson, we then consult scholarly and interpretive works, making certain that we move from merely hearing the text to setting the text in its proper context, which frequently adjusts our previously presumed meaning of the text. At this point we have determined two things: (1) What does this passage say to me? and (2) What did the author of this passage intend to say to his original listeners? Those may be two very different things, and each has validity as we prepare to preach. But the former cannot take precedence over the latter, or else, as mentioned in chapter 2, we fall into eisegesis rather than exegesis.

Having listened to the Word and then having studied it in acceptable scholastic fashion, we are prepared to wrestle with one of the questions from chapter 3: "So what?" What does this lesson have to do with the audience who will gather to hear us preach about it? I have found it helps me to consider individuals. Who is suffering or struggling at the moment? Who is facing some personal or professional crisis? Is there a helpful or hopeful word for them inherent in this text? It is also imperative to think of the congregation in the aggregate. What issues are we facing currently?

What programs, projects, or needs exist with which we are grappling on an ongoing basis? How does this lesson pertain to any of that? What's going on in the world around us? How bizarre it would have been on the Sunday immediately following 9/11 or the storms in Haiti for a minister to preach a sermon on stewardship! At some point, sermons must connect to the world in which they are heard. Read again the New Testament epistles. While filled with spiritual wisdom and theological depth, they also consistently relate to the life issues within the empire and to issues associated with the various communities to which the epistles were written.

Now the preacher has determined what the Scripture says to him or her, what it said in context, and how it relates to individuals, the congregation, or the world. The homework, however, is not yet complete. Now we have to decide how to speak this Word in a way that will seize the attention, deepen the understanding, and bring about some action by or within the audience. "How do I help them hear what I have discovered about this text and its relationship to church and world?" Remember our approach: *engage . . . exegete . . . apply*. With that formula in mind, one begins to write.

Writing can be both a laborious but also clarifying process. The first effort (rough draft) will be too lengthy. That is to be expected and perhaps even desired as the preacher labors to put on paper all that seems pertinent about the lesson(s). Once that is done, you are confronted with a key question. I first heard this stated by Dr. John Bergland, a personal friend, powerful preacher, and former professor of homiletics. Dr. Bergland said, "Good preachers always have to decide what not to say!" That is the key question: "Now that I have completed a rough draft of this sermon, what will I edit out? What will I not say?" It is not an easy exercise, given the fact that all we have learned via *lectio divina* and scholarly study, all we have discerned about the needs of individuals, congregations, and the world via observation, experience, and prayer, and all we have thus far written are treasured discoveries. Someone once said that the great novelist Thomas Wolfe (most famous for *Look Homeward, Angel*) was so protective of what he had written that anything an editor removed from one book would show up in his next one. Wolfe simply could not let go of that which he had created. It is a challenging task. And yet there comes a moment when the labors yield to clarification: What actually needs to be said in this one particular sermon, and how can it best be said? What is the central theme, and what else, though tasty, can be trimmed away as mere *adiaphora?*

The second writing therefore becomes a key communicative tool. The rough draft put your corpus of material on paper. The second writing is about editing and organizing. What genuinely needs to be said? How can it best be spoken to convey a central truth to the congregation and to make certain that they actually hear? What sort of language should be employed, given the fact that most congregants do not have access to a theological education and thus can become confused by some of our disciplinary language? At which point will a quote or anecdote help illustrate the central truth more vividly? At what point should an enjoyable story included in the rough draft be omitted from the final copy, noting that we preachers often hear intriguing stories and desire to pass them along quickly, sometimes trying to force them into a message where they do not actually fit? How much time do I spend lingering with the biblical text(s)? At what point do I begin to apply? How do I construct the segue? How often do I refer back to the text(s) during the application, thereby keeping the congregation centered in the timeless Word while exploring a specific word for their own time? How do I write an introduction that seizes their attention and a conclusion that ties the message up and either comforts the broken or inspires the listeners to action or both? This second writing is a process of clarification. It is the hard work of discerning what actually needs to be said and how best to say it. For some, the second writing is the final edition. For others, there is a third installment: either refining the manuscript into precise form, reducing the work to thorough and easy-to-follow notes, or committing the manuscript to outline format or to memory.

Once you have decided upon the most comfortable format, there comes the business of "owning it." By this, I simply mean you should now "live" with the sermon, pray about it, and practice it aloud (some even tape-record it and listen repeatedly). This is not a lecture to be read. It is a conversation among people of faith. Sometimes parishioners exit churches following worship, seize the preacher's hand, and utter the words, "This morning it felt as if you were talking directly to me." That is one of the greatest compliments a preacher can receive. Do not take it lightly. It means that you achieved what is desired in a homiletical event. You spoke the truth in a way that was accessible and pertinent, and our hearers need and deserve that.

To this point, we have discussed that which precedes the preaching event. Preparation to preach is not something that can be done hurriedly, not if you wish to do justice to the calling. Consider all that has been written about the process at this point. Can you do this effectively by sitting down Saturday night following dinner and asking, "What do I want to say tomorrow?" The answer to that question is obvious. As we noted earlier, the words that impress themselves on serious preachers are *time* and *effort.* Do your homework.

Believe in What You're Saying

This is simple and straightforward, and thus does not need a lot of unpacking. It is a basic rule of thumb within the world of communications that you cannot sell a product you wouldn't buy! My late father, a broadcast journalist and a public speaking instructor at a community college, frequently advised, "If you don't believe it, don't preach it." It was then and remains now powerfully important advice. Note that this is particularly challenging advice to lectionary preachers.

You will be pressured by congregants to address lessons or themes that do not inspire you. This is very different from addressing issues that frighten you. Most of us prefer to remain beside still waters, talking about topics that bring smiles, "amens," and warm compliments. But moments arrive when we are called upon to be prophetic—to speak a strong and biblical word about some controversial or pressing topic. In those moments, we enter the pulpit with faith but also with trembling, knowing that the reaction from our people will, in all likelihood, not be unanimously positive. Prophetic preaching requires courage. However, there will be moments when people pressure us to address topics that are outside our comfort zones not because they are prophetic, but rather because we are not theologically at home with them.

I recall a dear church member years ago who consistently asked me to preach about the doctrine of the Parousia. However, she had locked in her mind what she wanted me to say. She believed in a very specific understanding of the second coming, and she simply wanted her pastor to confirm it. She was an aged woman who lived near me, who regularly brought baked goods to my office and my parsonage, who was wonderfully affirming and maternal, and who would have given her last dime to the ministry of that congregation had she been asked. It was difficult on a personal level not to nod in her direction from the pulpit. However, she and I did not share a similar understanding of *parousia.* She believed that Jesus was coming soon to redeem the church and to receive the saints unto himself. I have a different understanding. I respect a variety of traditions, including her tradition, but am not limited to that particular interpretation of Scripture. I also realize that many deeply faithful people believe that the second coming occurred at the resurrection. Jesus lived. He died. He came again. Many others believe that the second coming occurred on the day of Pentecost. Jesus lived. He died. He was resurrected and ascended. But he also promised to send "a Comforter" (Jn 16:7). According to the Pentecost account in Acts 2, that is precisely what happened. There are many others of us who, issuing out of the Pentecost/*parousia* camp, believe that the comforting Spirit of God is not so much "to come" on some distant day, but rather "does come" this day and every day. I loved my church member, and I knew that she loved me, as a mother does her son. So I felt both pressure to oblige her and guilt for not doing so. And yet I could not preach what I did not believe. And when I preached a broader view, lifting up each of the traditions I just described and concluding with the Good News that God's Spirit comes to us always and everywhere, it did not feed the hunger she continued to express.

All this merely illustrates the sure truth that you, too, will feel pressured (sometimes even by the lectionary) to address themes outside your system of beliefs. If you do so, your discomfort with the theme will be transparent. People are wise and therefore quick to discern a lack of commitment on the part of a presenter. Even if you believe that the creation story, or the Noah story, or the Jonah story are myths, do not seek to preach as if you are quoting history or science. Look for the truth within the story, a truth too grand to be constrained by data or evidence. If you do not feel comfortable with a literal doctrine of this or that, find components of the doctrine that are applicable or relevant to contemporary living, and simply talk about those components. Or, better yet, find a different topic altogether. People desire—and deserve—an authentic word. They hunger to know something so real that the preacher can proclaim it with a confidence born of deep conviction. We owe them that. We owe ourselves that. We owe God that. So if you don't believe it, don't preach it!

Manage Your Manuscript

There is one additional consideration to reflect upon about the topic of style. The benefits of all the preparation you have done ultimately depend on what you do with the material once you stand before the people and they open their hearts to you. You have the goods in your hands. How will you deliver them?

As noted at the beginning of this chapter, many a strong message is derailed by inadequate presentation. And though substance always takes precedence over style, style certainly has the potential to put up a barricade against communicating substance if we are not careful. What we say matters most of all. But how we say it cannot be summarily dismissed. Putting people to sleep with strong scholarship ultimately prevents them access to the scholarship. Style matters. That being said, make note of a handful of simple suggestions.

People Are Not Engaged by a Sermon That Is Read to Them

If preaching is, in fact, a conversation between pulpit and pew, then imagine a conversation with a trusted friend who would only communicate with you by reading a script. She sits across the breakfast table from you talking about family, faith, politics, and life, but never looks you in the eyes. She never acknowledges that dialogue actually exists. Her only statements to you are read while you watch the top of her head as she gazes at the page. Soon enough, you would disengage and simply wish the visit to be concluded. Our congregations listen for a word from us spoken to them, not a word from a manuscript read to no one in particular.

This does not mean that manuscripts are taboo or that preachers who use them are ineffective communicators. It's *how*, not *if*, you employ the manuscript that matters. There is a profound difference between reading a work in a monotone, as if one were reciting cooking directions from a can of soup, and reading with inflection, passion, pacing, and an obvious commitment to the material being presented. Think of a performer who has just won an Oscar. She produces a piece of paper on which is written her acceptance speech. However, as she reads it, she frequently looks up at the audience, she smiles with excitement, she trembles with nervousness, she pauses to emphasize her indebtedness to the director or the producer, and she hurries to make certain no one is left off her list. The paper is there, but it is no more than a vehicle for expressing something too grand for the paper to contain. The written word does not mask the emotion or passion of the moment.

Or think of successful politicians. They read their speeches, not risking verbal missteps that the press or their opponents could use to their disadvantage. But they employ teleprompters so as not to appear to be reading (i.e., to establish a sense of dialogue with their listeners). And they use speech coaches who help them deliver scripted messages with power and humanity (or, again, with emotion and passion). Gifted politicians understand that people desire communication as opposed to lectures.

We preachers are called upon to give voice to the greatest story in human history. Nothing should mask the emotion and passion in telling that story. But it is masked when worshipers see nothing but the turning of pages in a notebook and the top of a person's head as he or she reads a theological homily that seems absolutely devoid of personal involvement with the topic. There is no question that it is justifiable to read one's manuscript . . . but only if we read it well.

Part of handling a manuscript is to know when to momentarily depart from it. Recall the second example from the beginning of this chapter. The man making the speech was careful to tell the audience what he wanted them to hear; thus did he stick to his written address. However, when the time came to illustrate his thesis by use of a potentially powerful personal story, he would have communicated far more effectively by turning away from the written pages and simply telling the story. It was, after all, his to tell. He could craft it as he chose. It was stored in his memory. There was no need to read the facts that he alone knew. Think of how intrigued we are when someone says, "You won't believe where I went last weekend . . .," or "I have to tell you about a home I visited . . .," or "The most inspiring thing happened to me at the grocery store . . .," or "I saw the funniest thing I've ever seen yesterday!" We lean forward in our seats to hear the story only they have to tell. But we would lean back in our seats if they were unable to convey their own anecdote without reading it from a page. Preaching from a manuscript is commendable. In fact, it is a credit to your labor of preparation. But there must be moments when you speak from the heart to the ears of your listeners, temporarily laying the printed page aside.

There Are Alternatives to Using a Manuscript If You Wish to Try Them

As previously noted, these options range from carrying a set of very full notes into the pulpit (which forces you to be more conversational and to employ eye contact) to using an outline with a few major points as road signs to keep you moving in the proper direction (again, which forces you to be more conversational and to employ eye contact) to memorizing your manuscript after you have completed the writing and editing. Either approach is acceptable and useful. The issue is not *what* you carry into the pulpit but instead *how* you use it once you get there. The faux pas of seeming professorial by leaning too heavily on a written manuscript is no more serious than the mistake of seeming ill-prepared and directionless by simply chattering without notes. What you carry into the pulpit should be a carefully crafted instrument that will assist you in making an informed, intelligent, and (hopefully) inspiring presentation to people who desire and deserve such.

It has been my personal practice through the years to write a rough draft, edit, rewrite a more clear and concise final copy, and then memorize. For me, it represents a journey from head to heart to lips. Admittedly, it does make me a rather dull dance partner on Saturday nights. I have to cloister on those evenings, reading the full manuscript aloud at least twice. At some point I stop reading the stories, as they need a less-scripted, more spontaneous feel about them. I will then commit myself to learning the didactic or prose portions between illustrations. I do not retire for bed until I can go through the manuscript from start to finish at least one time without looking at the papers. On Sunday mornings, I rarely consult the pages but do two more verbal walk-throughs of the sermon before actually preaching it. It represents a lot of labor, but it is the method that works best for me as I seek to project a sense of dialogue rather than monologue during the preaching event. Others achieve that sense of dialogue by effectively using notes, outlines, or manuscripts. Remember, it is not what we carry into the pulpit that matters, but rather how we use it.

Time Is a Reasonable Consideration

However, from congregation to congregation, "normal" lengths of sermons vary considerably. A former colleague of mine frequently is a summer guest lecturer at a seminary in Jamaica. His first year doing so, he was invited to preach at a local church. He took with him a sermon that had received rave reviews at the church where he was on staff. It was beautifully crafted, exegetically on target, and well illustrated. He threw himself into it with precision and passion. His style was more than acceptable. Back home in his own church, he would have received countless kudos, and rightfully so! However, after delivering his climactic closing line, he turned and sat down behind the pulpit, next to the host pastor. That pastor looked at my colleague and simply asked, "Is that it?" My friend's sermon had lasted for eighteen minutes. In that time he had effectively said what needed to be said about the text and how it applied to everyday living. However, he had addressed the text in a significantly different context of worship than he was used to. In that Jamaican church, the people expected a sermon to last forty-five minutes. That was their custom. To preach one-third of the customary time was almost insulting to that audience. In their minds, it communicated a lack of sufficient preparation, a lack of willingness to fully explain the biblical story, and a lack of respect for the needs of the people who had come to listen.

On the opposite end of the spectrum is a nationally famous (and properly respected) motivational speaker who appeared some time ago at the church I serve. He has authored numerous insightful and impressive books. He has much to say, all of which is both deep and vital. However, our folks are used to sermons that generally last about twenty-two minutes. That having been explained to the guest, he proceeded to speak for an hour. Had he been in the church in Jamaica, they may well have applauded. In our congregation, it was truly too much of a good thing. Several congregants confessed that they desired to exit midway through his presentation, but remained merely out of a sense of politeness.

The rules of thumb are basically two: (1) Say what needs to be said about text and topic. Do not rush past that which is crucial for the listener. If you speak with commitment and appropriate style, and if your material is strong, they will remain engaged. (2) Having said that, seek to be respectful of the worship culture within which you preach. If you are asked to preach in a "word and table" format of worship where the congregation is used to sermons that last fifteen to eighteen minutes, you will do no one any favors of faith by preaching for a half hour or more. In fact, in a sound-bite world, it is unlikely that many congregations will stick with any of us for that amount of time, however entertaining the preacher may be. The point is to understand the setting in which we proclaim God's word and to do within that setting that which best serves both the word and those who long to hear it. Time may not be of the essence, but it does matter in a significant way.

Imagine the Preaching Event from the Standpoint of the Listener

This may well be the single most important piece of advice of all. While writing and rehearsing the sermon, imagine what it would require for you to be open to and inspired by it were you sitting on a sanctuary pew. Think of yourself as a listener rather than a preacher. What would make you hear this word most authentically and effectively? Once we have determined what is most helpful to hearers, we are equipped to become far more helpful as speakers.

As we prepare our written sermons, special consideration needs to be given to language during the editing process. As we review what we have written up to this point, consider whether the language is inclusive or exclusive. Do we consistently use gender-specific imagery for God, effectively distancing listeners not of that gender? Are we intent on using helpful and appropriate language in describing demographical groups? Whereas we are sometimes called to speak a prophetic word (which occasionally has political implications), are our words partisan, alienating listeners rather than informing or inspiring them? Do we employ phrases that are too discipline-specific? Put another way, do we trot out theological language that serves more to obscure than to elucidate? All of us with seminary backgrounds can easily and naturally talk about "ecclesiology." However, does the use of the word assist our hearers who did not go to seminary? And if it doesn't, then perhaps we should substitute a more easily understandable phrase, such as "the study of what it means to be the church." Most of all, as we review the first draft, we should ask ourselves, Would it inspire me to hear this? Would I "get it"? Would I lean forward to listen? Would I be intrigued by this presentation? Would I want to hear more? Would it matter to me? Reviewing the manuscript by adopting the posture of a parishioner makes the second draft, or final copy, a far more meaningful document.

Another great way to see and hear ourselves from the viewpoint of those in the pew is to periodically watch videotaped recordings of our own preaching if we have access to the technology to do so. By so doing, I have often seen gestures I did not know I made which were, in fact, distracting, or segues that were cumbersome, or have heard the use of theological language that was too professional and thus not sufficiently accessible. We see what our worshipers see when we view a film. We hear each "uh" or "you know" too frequently repeated. We observe ourselves playing with our glasses or hitching our belts. We notice gestures that seem staged or unnatural or smiles that seem phony. We recognize when we should have stepped away from the manuscript and just talked to our people, as well as other moments when we needed to quit improvising and simply return to that which was prepared. Periodic film review of our preaching can be of great benefit when it comes to style. Also beneficial is to watch ourselves, from time to time, in the company of someone who is a gifted preacher and can help us spot both strengths to enhance and habits to improve or discard.

If our call to preach is *from* God but *for* people, then we need to prepare our sermons with the perspective of the hearers always in mind. Imagine the preaching event from the standpoint of the listener.

The story of faith is what matters most, but how it is proclaimed is also important. Substance is essential, but style is the vehicle by which substance is transported. When we have something as transformational as the Christian faith to talk about, it deserves to be addressed in a way commensurate with its sacred and inherent value.

CHAPTER 6

Models: Examples of Sermons that Engage, Exegete, and Apply

Included here are full sermon manuscripts that illustrate the approach I have been exploring in this book. These sermons use a variety of methods to engage the listeners, explore the biblical lessons in ways that represent fair and authentic exegetical method, and apply the exegeted materials to the specific particulars of (a) the world in which we live and/or (b) the distinctive setting for which the sermon was written. I include each with sincere gratitude to and respect for the preacher who submitted it. (Each sermon appears by permission of the author.)

Remember as you read these sermons that your task is not to agree with the particular social principle a preacher may be articulating, nor is it even to accept unilaterally his or her theological position (so long as the exegetical work is sound). As my children would say, "Don't get lost in the sauce." This book is about the work of homiletics. You can bring your own understanding of life issues and your own theological slant to the sermons you preach. Our task here, though, is to focus on how these preachers get the attention of their listeners, how they unfold the biblical texts, and ultimately how they connect the story to their hearers' stories. Consider how they address the "So what?" moments of their congregations.

Read. Reflect. Enjoy.

Where You From?
Genesis 28:10-22; John 1:43-51
Dr. Thomas Troeger, J. Edward and Ruth Cox Lantz Professor of Christian Communication, Yale (University) Divinity School.[1]

"Where you from?" How many times have you been asked that question in your life? And how many times have you asked it of others? On the surface it appears a simple ice breaker, a way of getting to know a stranger.

But several years ago, I became aware of the deeper dimensions behind the simple question, "Where you from?" My wife and I visited for one weekend the small hometown where I had grown up. I had not been back in many years. My parents had long ago moved away and were now dead. No one I had known while growing up still lived there. They had all moved away or died.

We strolled around town. It looked almost exactly as it had fifty years ago when I left for college. Schneider's Bakery was still at the four corners that featured the only traffic light in town. The cinema with its large marquee was down the street, only now it had been turned into a store. Everywhere I walked I had a story to tell.

"See that flat empty lot with a small ridge of earth about it? The town used to flood it with water in the winter to make it an ice rink."

"The house over there, on the shore where the lake empties into the river is where my friend, Jack, used to live. Summers we would get in his row boat and drift down to the dam, then row slowly back upstream."

"If you look northward along the lake, you can see a memorial marker. That was for a student who was killed in an automobile accident on the night of the senior prom. I'll never forget how people sobbed at commencement."

"The white clapboard house attached to the church: that's where I was baptized when I was sixteen. I remember Jake Schaeffer, my high school history teacher, holding the bowl of water while Reverend Weld's wet hand touched my forehead three times."

One story after another tumbled out of me. Most of them were fond memories, but some of them were ugly and painful, especially the racial and religious stereotypes that the town folk sometimes expressed about different kinds of people who they were grateful did not live there. As we drove away at the end of the weekend, I recall watching the lake and the hills and the steeple of my childhood church disappearing in my rear view mirror, the same way they had vanished fifty years earlier. But I now realized the town was still alive inside me, through the memories of people and stories and events and through the ways they had shaped who I became and what I believe in and how I speak and act. A lot of it was to the good, but some of it, especially the prejudice and the parochialism, were not.

"Where you from?" The question is more than an ice breaker. What are the memories of people and stories and events that for good and for ill shaped who you are and what you believe in and how you speak and act?

If you asked Nathanael, who appears in today's gospel, "Where you from?" he would answer, "From Cana." We know Nathanael is from Cana because later in the Gospel of John we are told Cana was his hometown. Cana must have been like my hometown, and perhaps yours as well. Cana had shaped Nathanael in some good ways because Christ describes him as someone "'in whom there is no deceit.'" But Cana also must have planted some prejudice in Nathanael. For when Philip tells Nathanael about "'Jesus son of Joseph from Nazareth,'" Nathanael immediately responds, "'Can anything good come out of Nazareth?'" The words shoot out of his mouth, the way a deeply ingrained prejudice usually does.

Nazareth was a tiny village in Galilee. It had no significant highway nearby, and it possessed only one flowing spring so that cisterns were used to collect adequate water. Nathanael's hometown of Cana was also in Galilee. His snide comment may reflect local prejudice, the kind of thing my friends and I expressed when we were children by saying someone was from "Hicksville." Whatever the exact cause of Nathanael's disparaging remark, I am impressed with how Philip answers him. Philip does not try to reason Nathanael out of his prejudice. Prejudice is generally not very responsive to reason because it is not rooted in reason to begin with. Instead, Philip says to Nathanael, "Come and see." Three words. A simple invitation. "Come and see." That is the way Philip opens Nathanael to possibilities that he otherwise would rule out from the start. Philip models how to answer those who are skeptical about Jesus. Do not try to argue people into following Christ. Invite them. "Come and see."

When Jesus sees Nathanael approaching, the first words out of his mouth are not "Can anything good come out of Cana?" Instead, he welcomes Nathanael with words of affirmation: "'Here is truly an Israelite in whom there is no deceit!'" The contrast between Nathanael's snarky question and Christ's hospitality reveal to us the qualitative difference between our tangled prejudices and the grace of God that reaches out to call forth whatever is best in us.

Christ's generous spirit does not immediately win Nathanael over. Instead of appreciating the grace Christ extends toward him, Nathanael continues to sound skeptical: "'Where did you get to know me?'" But the minute Christ tells about seeing him under the fig tree, Nathanael does an abrupt about face: "'Rabbi, you are the Son of God! You are the King of Israel!'" John the gospel writer is compressing into a very brief exchange, the wonder of what can happen when human prejudice and skepticism encounter the grace, hospitality and visionary spirit of Christ. No matter where we are from, no matter how it has shaped us for ill as well as for good, the grace of Christ has the capacity to draw us beyond the limitations of our hometown mentality. Nathanael has moved from "'Can anything good come out of Nazareth?'" to a confession of faith in Christ, and Christ has come out of Nazareth!

Now that Nathanael has moved from disparagement and skepticism to faith, Christ tells him, "'You will see heaven opened and the angels of God ascending and descending upon the Son of Man.'" The vision Christ offers is based on Jacob's dream at Bethel in Genesis 28. Jacob dreams of a ladder between heaven and earth on which angels ascend and descend. To understand the richness of what Christ promises Nathanael, I turn to interpretations of Jacob's dream that Jewish rabbis have developed.

When Jacob lies down to sleep, the Hebrew version of the text that the Rabbis used, says that he made a pile of stones for a pillow, but when Jacob awakes the pillow is a single stone. Some rabbis have suggested that the individual stones had started arguing about which one of them was most worthy to support the head of the patriarch. But when the heavenly vision appeared, when the holiness of God drew near, the fragmented creation was restored as one stone. So when Christ invokes the story of Jacob's ladder, he is telling Nathanael that he will find his own fragmented self restored to wholeness.

The rabbis have also noted that in Jacob's dream the angels are "ascending and descending" the ladder. The rabbis are surprised at the word order, thinking that angels come from God (descending) before they return to God (ascending). But since the word "ascending" appears first in the story, the rabbis conclude it might be a way of indicating God had already sent Jacob strength, and he had not been aware of it when he was awake. Or perhaps the ascending angels represent the profoundest prayers and yearnings of Jacob's heart that are then answered by the descending angels. So when Christ invokes the story of Jacob's ladder, he is telling Nathanael that he will find God responding to the profoundest yearnings of his heart.

Finally, the rabbis have noted that when Jacob decides to lie down, he does not choose the place because it is sacred ground. The only reason

Jacob settles there is because night has come and he has been on the run and is exhausted. But when he arises, after the vision granted in his dream, Jacob has an astounding realization: "'Surely the Lord is in this place – and I did not know it.'" So when Christ invokes the story of Jacob's ladder, he is telling Nathanael that he will become aware that God was with him even when he did not know it.

What is true for Nathanael is true for us as well. When we follow Christ, our fragmented life is gathered into wholeness, our profoundest longings receive a gracious response, and we come to realize that God has been with us even when we did not know it. This is the abundance of life that Christ offers Nathanael when he says, "'You will see heaven opened and the angels of God ascending and descending upon the Son of Man.'" This is the abundance of life that Christ offers us.

Christ often extends such abundance of life through strangers and people who come from places that we disparage as vigorously as Nathanael did when he asked "'Can anything good come out of Nazareth?'" Consider what Nathanael would have missed if he had not responded to Philip's invitation, "'Come and see.'" Consider what we will miss if we do not respond to Philip's invitation, "'Come and see:'"

Wholeness, Fulfilled longing,

The divine presence.

Would you want to miss these?

I don't think so.[1]

Born in Perplexity
Luke 1:26-38

> *Dr. Lillian Daniel, senior minister, First Congregational Church, United Church of Christ, Glen Ellyn, Illinois. Dr. Daniel has taught preaching at Yale Divinity School and Chicago Theological Seminary. This sermon was preached in Glen Ellyn, 18 December 2005 and appeared in* Journal for Preachers.

You notice that at the end of this extraordinary dialogue between Mary and the angel, she is restrained in how she describes her emotional state, in what she commits to. Having offered herself up in service to the Lord, having said "Let it be with me according to your word," she does not go on to say this: "Oh, yes. And now I understand everything."

No, the passage does not ever downplay the fact that Mary is perplexed, and that Christ's conception is downright confusing, even to his mother. Why, Mary is perplexed even before the angel tells her that she is pregnant.

"And he came to her and said, 'Greetings, favored one! The Lord is with you.' But she was much perplexed by his words and pondered what sort of greeting this might be." So Mary is perplexed from the moment the angel first greets her.

I am reminded of the popular line from the movie *Jerry Maguire*, when the lady he is declaring his love to finally responds to his lengthy speech to inform him, "You had me at 'hello.'"

Except that Mary might have concluded this whole dialogue with the angel a bit differently: "You perplexed me at 'hello.'" She begins, and I would say concludes, this scene thoroughly and totally perplexed, from hello to goodbye.

As one who spends much of life in such a state, I take comfort. I see this passage as a great anthem, a symphony, in honor of those of us who move forward not in clarity, not in certainty, not in single-mindedness, but with perplexity. We're the ones at the back of the orchestra, hoping but doubting we're in the right place, playing with gusto nonetheless.

For perplexity, as a state of mind, is hugely underrated in our sure-footed society. Think about what we want in a leader these days. We want someone who knows what he wants, is clear on what she thinks, makes a decision and makes it quickly. Think how strange it would be to hear a news anchor describe the president as confused. Imagine it. "In his radio address to the nation this week, the president, when looking at the state of the nation, the state of the world, the attacks from opposing political parties as well as various natural disasters and diseases facing the world, had this response: 'Quite frankly, I am perplexed.'"

But sometimes I wish we could hear that. For there's a news flash right here in the Bible: the most important woman in the world, the one who is about to give birth to the son of God, the one who will have to tell her beloved news of a pregnancy that will bring scandal to their new life, the one who will sit at the foot of the cross heroically suffering her son into eternity, the one who now as a young girl will have to have the strength to travel long distances in miles and even greater distances in faith, begins her adventure in a state of perplexity. From the moment the angel greets her, she is confused.

To me, that's enormously freeing. I think people of faith should rejoice in it. I don't mean to make too much of this one narrative detail, but imagine how the story changes if you had Mary adding a few upbeat, clarifying remarks like this at the end: "Thanks for the update, Gabe. Consider me up-to-date and informed. I'm moving ahead with total clarity. But I expect to be kept in the loop on any upcoming developments. I'll take it from here." Imagine how the cocky bravado of office chatter would change the story.

Instead, in a much richer story, our hero makes no claim to understand it; there is no surefooted statement to sum it all up. Mary makes no comment to indicate the confusion and perplexity have lifted at all. She simply offers herself up to God, just as she is; confusion, perplexity, and all. Because apparently, when it comes to leaders of God's revolution here on earth, a little perplexity and confusion is exactly what God is looking for.

But in a world that wants answers, and wants them now, can we believe in a God who can live with our questions?

So often in the life of the church, we look around from pew to pew and wonder, "Is every body else here getting something that I don't get?"

Never mind the simple Sunday morning logistical issues of when you are supposed to stand up and when are you supposed to sit down, or whether or not you are supposed to clap, how you are supposed to know which book to open when in the service, or where you are supposed to park. The confusion there is obvious, and usually the answers, while not obvious, can be rooted out over time.

But isn't there a deeper inner confusion we feel? A worry that perhaps everyone gets something we don't. We sit in church looking at our neighbor and wondering, "Do they ever question any of this stuff, because I sure do."

And then in another seat up the aisle, someone else might be wondering, "Does everyone question this stuff except for me? And if my faith is steady, does that make me question-impaired? Perhaps in my lack of confusion, I'm confused . . ."

But then we all sit up straight, open our worship bulletins decisively, and with a churchy certainty, try to look as though we are people who are not perplexed.

To which I would like to offer this small comfort: if the mother of God got to be perplexed, you can be too. In fact, let's take perplexity out of the old broom closet, dust it off, shine it up, and put it out on the mantle-piece in the middle of the ecclesiological living room, because a little perplexity can be a wonderful thing in the life of faith.

For that matter, let's stop whitewashing Mary into some paragon of girlish obedience, and see her instead as the complicated woman she was, a person of complexity, a person of perplexity. How could she be anything else?

Given that Mary found herself in conversation with an angel who was telling her that as a virgin, she would give birth to the Son of Man, we can presume that her questions were both big and substantial. We ought to delight that the Scripture doesn't downplay that, but tells us up front that she's perplexed and then does not wipe that away. As the conversation continues, she stays perplexed, asking "How can it be?" just like we would. And even in her perplexity, God doesn't drop her. Rather, God chooses her.

Two thousand years later, we sit here in Advent, waiting for the birth of a baby who has already been born, waiting for the son of God who reverses life, death, and reshapes time itself. And every now and then, we too are perplexed. We ask our angels, "How can it be?" And God doesn't drop us either.

It almost makes you wonder: could God be out there looking for the perplexed?

For why not take a minute to imagine what Mary would have been if she had not been perplexed when greeted by an angel. Without perplexity, Mary would have to have been one of three things: unaware, a "know it all," or simply not a good choice for God's plan.

First, if the Scripture had not indicated to us that she was confused by all of this, we'd have to ask ourselves: did she even realize she was talking to an angel? Did she hear what the angel was saying? Did she get it? Her per-plexity tells us, as readers two thousand years later, that she grasped the divine magnitude of it all. She understood enough to understand that she did not understand.

If that makes sense. Which it doesn't. Which it shouldn't. Which is my point.

But secondly, if Mary had not been perplexed, and the Gospel writer had not been kind enough to include this detail, we would have been left thinking Mary was a "know it all." And nobody likes a "know it all." If Mary had responded to the angel with a bored, "So here you finally are," or with a knowing wink, we would be left annoyed that God would choose some spiritual "know it all," instead of a real person, who, in the face of divine mystery, is as confused as the rest of us.

And lastly, without her perplexity, Mary would not have been a solid choice for mother of God, because if you're going on that kind of adventure, you had better have a sense of confusion, wonder, questioning, and perplexity, or you won't make it.

Because this was not a journey for the "smartest kid in the class," or the "answer guy" at work, or the "know it all" who cuts off all ideas with the answers at every meeting. This was a job. Rather, this was a calling, for a person whose spirit was open. Wide open. Perplexity leaves the spirit open to be touched by God.

Sometimes it's in admitting we don't have all the answers, that suddenly we can hear a whisper from another place. Sometimes, in admitting that we don't get it, we open ourselves up to get something from God. Sometimes when we stop talking and giving ourselves the answers to our own questions, we allow ourselves to be filled up with something new.

With Jesus even.

Who chose someone who was confused to bring him into this world.

I'm guessing that your questions can't be bigger than Mary's. I'm guessing that when she said, "How can it be . . .," she was still more confused than I'll ever be. Look at what she had just heard.

If Jesus could live in someone who had questions like that, surely he can live in you too.

It turns out that in the end, in order to be part of God's plan, you don't actually have to understand it all.

But you could take a second look at a confused teenage girl who in the face of a divine dilemma and a perplexing pregnancy could still say this: "Here am I, the servant of the Lord; let it be with me according to your word."

Build Houses, Plant Gardens
Jeremiah 29:1, 4-7; Luke 17:1-19
Dr. Jon M. Walton, First Presbyterian Church, New York, New York, October 10, 2010.

In recent weeks, the news has been anything but good. Everywhere you turn there is bad news.

In Luvungi, in the Eastern Congo, there are reports of atrocities: over 200 women, including elderly women, have been raped by combatants there, only a few miles from the location of UN peacekeeping troops.

In Hungary, a vast industrial spill is sending caustic sludge toward the Danube River.

In Pakistan, a shaky regime still reeling from the flooding of late August is rightly incensed at our government after American troops last week conducted a helicopter raid on a border post and killed three Pakistani soldiers.

Closer to home, we have been shaken this early semester by the suicide of a young man whose private and intimate encounter with another student was streamed live on the Internet by his roommate using a hidden webcam. And this weekend a gang in the Bronx sodomized a young gay man and terrorized others on a homophobic rant.

Then there is the horror of a trial in Connecticut where a husband was beaten with a baseball bat and a wife and two daughters were raped and burned to death in a fire.

And I have not even mentioned that American military casualties in Afghanistan this week exceeded 1,200 young lives, and who knows how many Afghanis have died? I don't want to read the newspaper anymore or listen to the news in the evening. It's too discouraging. Whether it be *world* or *local* events, there seems to be little but bad news.

And I don't think it's going to get much better if the political scene is any measure. The state of public debate about the issues that are shaping our country in this election year, in this time of economic challenge and international unrest, are pitiful. Candidates for office are not talking about the issues. They are offering slogans and sound bites. I suppose one might ask, "So what else is new?" But I despair at our New York gubernatorial race. I am amazed at poor Christine O'Donnell's best hope of being elected to the Senate from Delaware resting on the affirmation that *she is not a witch*. How sad is the state of American leadership when that is the level of public discourse on critical issues in such a crucial time?

Things are just not right in the world, and one cannot help but feel discouraged by the abundance of bad news that inundates us every day. It takes its toll on our spirit. We may well wonder whether there is a God who is keeping an eye on things.

It's not the first time that people of faith have looked at current events and wondered where the signs of hope might be. In Jeremiah's time, Israel was in captivity.

Conquered by King Nebuchadnezzar, its leading citizens had been taken away from Jerusalem and transplanted to Babylon. It was not the same kind of captivity that Israel had known in Egypt. Not slavery as such. The captives were allowed to keep their families and communities together. Public gatherings and communal worship were permitted. But there was no temple, and they longed for the home where they had left behind many friends, all of their possessions, and their holy places. Psalm 137 tells us of the sadness they bore: "By the rivers of Babylon, there we sat down and there we wept when we remembered Zion. On the willows there we hung up our harps. For there our captors asked us for songs, and our tormentors asked for mirth, saying, 'Sing us one of the songs of Zion.'"

It's hard to go on when you live in the past, missing what once was, longing for days that can be no more. What was it like to have lived in such a time as that Babylonian Exile? The only thing I can imagine in modern-day experience to compare would be what people in New Orleans have experienced in the wake of Hurricane Katrina fleeing from their homes, returning to destruction. Or the experience of people in the Gulf Coast region after the Deepwater Horizon oil spill, or perhaps what the people of Haiti are still experiencing in the wake of the earthquake that shook it in January and Igor's additional insult this past August. They are people who feel cut off from the past and discouraged about the future, and for good reason.

We know what this feeling is like in our own experience, what it is to live in the past and not be able to move forward. It's remembering those days when the kids were first starting out at school instead of heading off to college. It's five years ago when building that summer place upstate seemed like such a good idea, but which now is such a financial burden that you wonder how you ever talked yourself into going ahead with it.

It's the empty seat in the pew, the one that was always filled by someone you loved who is no longer there anymore. It's thumbing through the wedding album, or watching the DVD they made of that day, and realizing that things are not as good between you now as they were then. The warmth of affection has changed, the excitement about the future is clouded. And some days, well . . .

We get lost, sometimes, living in the past, remembering how it was, or maybe it's being lost, wishing for something that never was, we just imagined it was. We can be so lost in our own reverie that we cannot find our way back. Funny how our lives look so much better in the rearview mirror than they do through the front windshield when it's coming on.

I suppose that's what was going on with Israel in exile in 597 BC. Everything in the past looked so good, so peaceful and right. Everything in Babylon seemed so wrong, and they could not seem to make for themselves a home in captivity. It is a real problem to be stuck like that.

Over the summer I read Tracy Kidder's book *Strength in What Remains* (New York: Random House, 2009), the remarkable story of Deogratias, a refugee from the ethnic violence in Burundi and the genocide in Rwanda who came to the United States virtually penniless in 1993 and did what so many refugees do. He got by on his wits. Barely, at times, but he made do. He lived for a while as a squatter in a rat- and roach-infested tenement, delivering groceries at service entrances on the Upper East Side. He lived with homeless people who spoke his language in Central Park, hungry much of the time, living hand to mouth.

The story is incredible. Were it not true, it would be impossible. Deo goes to school and finds his way to (of all places) Columbia University, where he earns his undergraduate degree in philosophy and is haunted by his memories of a war-torn Burundi. Though he is now an American citizen, he visits Burundi often and bears in his heart a desire to do something worthwhile and enduring in his native land. He has established a health clinic and wellness program in Kigutu, a place where Tutsis and Hutus can come for treatment in peace and safety.

Tracy Kidder, in writing of this remarkable man whom he has described so powerfully, says, "In the end, it's neither forgetting the past nor dwelling on the past that has worked for [Deo]. For him, the answer has been remembering and acting."

I doubt that the people of Israel's loneliness and memories were any less sorrowful or haunting than were Deo's memories of his lost country and troubling past. Which is why God's instruction to Israel is so remarkable.

"Thus says the Lord of Hosts, the God of Israel to all . . . whom I have sent into exile from Jerusalem to Babylon. Build houses, plant gardens, take wives, seek the welfare of the city and pray for it." In other words, get on with life. It's a command, not as fascile as "bloom where you are planted," but an imperative to take seriously the possibility that God can be found *in exile* every bit as much as *at home*. That even in Babylon God had not abandoned them. "Get on with life," then, God said. "Build houses, plant gardens, take wives, seek the welfare of the city and pray for it." Let the future take care of itself. Do not waste today.

I think about people I have known who are always waiting for the right occasion, the timely development, the stars to align before they can write the book that they have always had in their mind, or start the project they want to accomplish, or make the change that never seems appropriate right now.

In that sense, I suppose all of us have a *Bucket List*, as it were, a list of things we would like to do before we kick the bucket and life ends. For Jack Nicholson and Morgan Freeman in the movie of that name, the list included skydiving and getting tattoos on their hands, climbing the pyramids, eating dinner at Chevre d'Or in France, seeing the Taj Mahal, and riding a motorcycle on the Great Wall of China. But doing a lot of daredevil things or recapturing a youth of missed opportunities is not exactly what God is urging Israel to do.

What Israel thought was that life was on hold. That God was back in Jerusalem and nowhere to be found. They had left the temple behind, and surely God must be there too. The problem was that for the foreseeable future, there was no going back. So what were they to do? They spent their days lost in the past, remembering the way things were, unable to move forward into what was yet to be.

God had to tell them that they did not need to return to Jerusalem in order to worship God and live life. Life had changed. But life was worth living, even in Babylon. So "build houses," God said, "plant gardens, take a wife, seek the welfare of the city. This is the life you have, so this life you must live. Now get on with it."

What happens when you do such a thing? When you so lay claim to the love and grace of God that even though you are not where you want to be, you discover that where you are may be enough.

I've told this story before, but I told it on Memorial Day weekend last year, and none of you were here, so you will all be hearing it for the first time. And if you were here, well, a good story is worth telling more than once. It's the story of Vedran Smailovic, the cellist of Sarajevo.

Vedran Smailovic was principal cellist in the Sarajevo Philharmonic Orchestra. And while many heard him play in the symphony hall of Sarajevo, he is most remembered for playing in a hole.

On May 27, 1992, bombs were dropping on Sarajevo. And one fell outside of Smailovic's window, landing on hungry people standing in line for bread. The bombs killed twenty-two men, women, and children of the city and left a hole in the street filled with their blood.

The next day and every day thereafter for twenty-two days, Vedran Smailovic emerged from his apartment dressed in concert tails. He placed a stool in the bomb crater and at other strategic points in the city and played his cello. He played a song of life. He played a song of hope stronger than fear, of good greater than evil, of bravery overpowering cowardice, of life overwhelming death. He played as an exile in the center of Babylon, claiming that time and that crater and his city as a place where even God might be made known. It was Albinoni's *Adagio in G Minor* for strings that he played, but it was a prayer that he played as well, a prayer that said life can overcome death, and hope triumphs over the worst despair can do.

I don't know what it is that might be keeping you from living your life more fully. Whether it's some fear that the timing is not right, or the stars are not aligned, or you're not in the right place, or your parents would disapprove even though they are long gone, or you don't have enough money to do it, or you have too much to do it, or you're too old, or too young. There are a lot of Babylons in which to be exiled.

Maybe it's finally talking about that thing that you cannot discuss in your marriage, or maybe it's affirming in your life that truth about yourself that you have always known is true but couldn't acknowledge. Maybe it's getting a grip on that which has a grip on you, the alcohol, the drugs, the destructive habit that is stealing your life.

I don't know what it is that is holding you back. But you do. And I don't know when might be a better time to deal with it than now. But maybe you do. What I do know is that in a time when God's people seemed least ready to lay hold of their future, God said, "Build houses, plant gardens, take wives, seek the welfare of the city." Get on with living. For what seems to us *least* likely, in God's economy, is often what is *most* likely. And God sometimes calls us to do what we feel least prepared to do, which is to get on with life, to embrace the day, and to discover in so doing that God is precisely *there*.

A Triangular Faith
Matthew 2:1-12

Rev. Dr. Sam Wells, vicar, St. Martin-in-the-Fields Anglican Church, London.

I vividly remember a train journey I made when I was around twenty years old. It was a bright spring day, and I got on the train in London. Gradually my heart beat more smoothly and my lungs expanded as we left the city and the suburbs and reached the open green fields and patterned hedgerows and started to see grazing cows and sheep. As the train drew near my destination, my eyes began to fill with tears, and a whole host of memories pulled and prodded and shook me, like a gaggle of lively children demanding attention.

Returning to that part of the English countryside evoked a complex pattern of emotions for me. My mother died a slow and agonizing death when I was eighteen. Living with my father in my parents' house was too intense, so a few months after the funeral, I'd come to live in this beautiful part of the world. I had a job as a driver for a man who often travelled 200 miles a day. He liked to use his time in the car for writing letters. He was a fascinating person, and we had a lot of searching and memorable conversations. It was a time of serious spiritual growth for me. Several people met locally at 5:30 every weekday morning for an hour of devotion and silence, and it was the first time I'd been exposed to the rhythm of prayer shaping my morning, noon, and night. But while I was finding a new intimacy with God, there was a deep loneliness and sadness as well. I used to take my employer's dog for solitary walks across the hills and dales, and became used to being alone on the long summer evenings.

That train journey back, a couple of years later, was the first time I can remember feeling the powerful resonance of place. All the perplexity and complexity of that summer of grief and discovery was soaked into those hillsides and open fields. When you're happy, you remember the people you were happy with. But when you're sad, you take solace in the landscape and quiet places, because they become your friends.

The second chapter of Matthew's Gospel awakens us to three places that shape the imagination of his Gospel. Matthew places great store by the fulfillment of the Scripture. Each of the key locations in Matthew chapter 2 is accompanied by a suitable quotation from the Old Testament. As we stand at the beginning of the new year, I invite you to inhabit these three locations that mark the territory of the Gospel.

The first place is Bethlehem. Bethlehem is a place of long-buried mystery and possibility. It was previously known as Ephrath, and the prophet Micah has an echoing word that says, "O Bethlehem of Ephrathah, who are one of the little clans of Judah, from you shall come forth for me one who is to rule in Israel, whose origin is from of old, from ancient days." The great King David had come from Bethlehem, but it had been more or less a thousand years since anything much had happened there, so no one was holding their breath.

Bethlehem is six miles from Jerusalem. When the Wise Men crossed the desert from the east, they took for granted that the new king would be born in Jerusalem. The star directed them towards Bethlehem, but they thought the star was wrong. They went to Herod's palace, and there they found scribes who knew the ancient prophecy. But to turn around from Herod's palace and head to Bethlehem, the Wise Men had to unlearn a number of the expectations that had made them wise. The savior was not going to affirm the status quo. The savior was not going to be born in a seat of power. The savior was not going to be greeted with universal acclaim, even from his own people. The savior was not going to change the world overnight. The Wise Men weren't just wrong about the star—they were wrong about everything the star represented.

But because Herod had now learned of Jesus' birth from the Wise Men, Bethlehem suddenly became a place of danger. Herod had every male child under two years old killed. So suddenly the place of obscurity, of legend, of long-lost possibility, had become a place of terror. I wonder what the shepherds thought about this terrible slaughter. Was this the good news of joy and peace the angels had brought them that starry, starry night? Or did they curse the day they'd seen the sky filled with angels, because everything since had been tragedy and cruelty and murderous butchery?

Many of us have known a place of tranquility suddenly become a place of danger. As the new year begins, I wonder what might be a place of danger for you. I wonder where might be a place that your faith, your witness, your very existence seems to be a challenge, a threat, an infuriating and inflammatory provocation that evokes malice, hatred, and violence from others. Bethlehem, the place of danger. I wonder where Bethlehem is going to be for you this year.

Just in time, Joseph had a dream, and took his wife and child away in the middle of the night. There's a certain irony about where he went.

Herod's deeds in wiping out the newborn children recall the actions of Pharaoh in the story of Moses. Remember, baby Moses wouldn't have ended up as a basket case floating down the Nile if Pharaoh hadn't been set on murdering all the Hebrew boys. So for Joseph of Nazareth to take his family down to Egypt in the face of Herod's brutality looks like exchanging the devil for the deep blue sea. But a lot had changed since Moses had led his people out of Egypt 1,500 years before. A baby born in the shadows but called the light of the world was no threat to the Egyptians now. The aging Herod had only a few more years to live, and it wasn't unreasonable for the holy family to keep out of the limelight for a little while.

Egypt represented a place of escape. Just as Bethlehem had flipped over from obscurity to danger, so now Egypt had flipped over from danger to escape. There's a lot in most of us that's longing to escape. Some escapes are very good ones. The ability to relax, and play, and enjoy adventure can be important and creative kinds of renewal. Other escapes, like Joseph and Mary's, are vital ways of staying alive, or staying sane. Many people dream of an exotic vacation, or stare intently at a bottle of sleeping pills, or identify intimately with a celebrity or a sports team, firmly desiring that this alternative reality will alleviate the pressure from their present one. And some escapes aren't really escapes at all, and could better be described as exile, because in order to preserve your life, you leave a place you love, and abide for a time in a place where you don't want to be, until your circumstances change for the better.

As the new year begins, I wonder what might be a place of escape for you. I wonder where it might be that you run away to, and whether that hiding place is one of desperate preservation, or anxious denial, or healthy renewal. I wonder what part of your soul or body is in danger right now and needs Joseph's guiding hand to lead it to a place of escape. I wonder what it is that deep down you might be running away from. I wonder if part of you is in exile and doesn't want to be where you are at all. Egypt, the place of escape. I wonder where Egypt is going to be for you this year.

Joseph was quite the dreamer. He had another dream in Egypt, and it led him back to the land of Israel, and eventually to Galilee, in the north of the country, where he settled in Nazareth. Unlike Bethlehem and Egypt, Nazareth had no special connection to a significant moment in Israel's story. This was not a place with any expectation that something remarkable was to happen: and as far as we know, nothing remarkable did. Except this was where the character of the Son of God was formed, filled, shaped, and deepened. Nazareth is the third location of Joseph and Mary's journey. It's where the story of Matthew chapter 2 reaches its conclusion. Nazareth is a place of nurture. Jesus spent all but a few years of his life there, as far as we know. Nazareth was the place that formed him for the times of courage and sacrifice that lay ahead of him.

As the new year begins, I wonder what might be a place of nurture for you. I wonder whether the place you're spending most of your time is truly a place of nurture. I wonder whether the place you've spent most of your life is truly place of nurture. I wonder what are the parts of your soul that need nurturing this year—maybe parts that take a long time to grow, need a lot of encouragement, are still to find fruit and fertile soil. Nazareth, the place of nurture. I wonder where Nazareth is going to be for you this year.

Bethlehem, Egypt, Nazareth. If you set the three locations out geographically, they form a triangle—with Egypt bottom left, Bethlehem bottom right, and Nazareth at the top. Picture that triangle for a moment. I wonder where you would place yourself in that triangle right now. I wonder whether your life would be near one corner, tending toward danger, with perhaps a little bit of nurture. Or near another corner, maybe nurture, with a little bit of escape. And I wonder whether you're expecting, in the year to come, to find yourself in a different place in the triangle to where you were last year.

As you think about your faith, as you stand before God, I wonder where you think God is in this triangle. When you turn to God and consider your life before God, where do you stand? Is God with you in danger? Does God lead you into danger? Or do you see your life and ministry as fundamentally placing you in positions of danger just like Jesus? Is faith largely a matter of escape—of retreat into a spiritual world, where earthly pressures are less depressing and overwhelming, and where hope, and peace, and freedom are close at hand? Or is God, for you, mainly about nurture, growth, and understanding, with few moments of revelation but a lot of gentleness, and slow realization, and deepening of character?

And finally think about the life and mission of the church. Is the church called to be in Bethlehem, constantly in places of danger and sacrifice facing fear and fury? Or is it called to be in Egypt, far away from such troubled territory, offering an oasis of calm and security and keeping its head down lest there be any trouble? Or is the church called to be in Nazareth, slowly cherishing, and nurturing, and fostering, and being present as the kingdom emerges before its eyes?

As a pastor I find that a great deal of disagreement and unhappiness in congregations arises from the fact that members have significantly different understandings of where they are in the triangle, and where their church is called to be. You can imagine that a person who comes to worship longing for an oasis of escape from their chaotic life is easily horrified when the message they're getting is that we're all called to Bethlehem, to face danger with Christ. But I believe my role as a pastor isn't to push, nudge, or persuade people into Nazareth, Egypt, or Bethlehem. It's to craft a whole community that lives within this triangle, sharing one another's dangers, and oases, and learnings, and helping each other to meet God in each one. The secret is to stay within the triangle. And I think that's why my eyes filled with tears those years ago when I went back to a place where I'd known grief, and escape, and growth. They were tears of joy and sadness, of crossing a threshold back into a place of more intense life, a place I might now call the kingdom of God. I was coming back into a place that had, in different ways, represented danger, escape, and nurture. What I was doing was reentering the triangle.

I hope that's what you do when you cross the threshold of this chapel on a Sunday morning. I hope it's what you're doing right now as you're taking a step into this brave new year. It will have danger, and escape, and growth.

May the danger be because your faith and your God are a threat to the Herods of today. May the escape be a time of preservation and renewal for greater tasks—tasks closer to who you truly are and what you were truly made for—tasks yet to be shouldered, when the time is right. And may the nurture be a time of growth and tenderness at the heart of the holy family.

Happy New Year. You're entering the triangle. The triangle where Jesus abides. God bless you.

The Tree of Life
Revelation 22:1-2
Dr. Brad Braxton, distinguished visiting scholar, McCormack Theological Seminary, Chicago.

I live in a neighborhood on the south side of Chicago where there are several magnificent trees. Their wide trunks and towering branches indicate that they are ancient residents of our neighborhood. Decades, maybe even centuries, before we moved in, they were already there.

As I stood recently gazing at some of those towering trees, I was reminded that trees play a central role in Christianity. Trees serve as landmarks on the journey of fallen and redeemed humanity. According to the Scriptures, the first tree in the history of salvation was in the Garden of Eden. Dr. Gardner Taylor, the dean of American preachers, once suggested Eden's divine landlord told Adam and Eve that they had the run of the whole place—except for one tree. Adam and Eve were explicitly instructed not to touch the tree of the knowledge of good and evil. But temptation crawled on its belly into the precincts of paradise, placing before Adam and Eve an offer they could not, or would not, refuse.

Because of their disobedience at the first tree, Adam and Eve broke the conditions of their lease, and God evicted them from paradise. The first tree was in Eden. It was the tree of shame. At that tree, our feet stumbled, and we fell from grace.

Because of the tragedy at the first tree, there would eventually be a second tree. On a dark Friday, on a skull-shaped hill outside the city walls of Jerusalem, Jesus hung from the sixth to the ninth hour on a tree. His bruised body, convulsing with pain, stood affixed between heaven and hell on that tree.

Humanity's disobedience at the first tree would be consummated generations later at the second tree as Rome visited unspeakable violence upon Jesus. The second tree was a heinous spectacle of imperial violence, demonstrating how costly it is when prophets *justly* challenge *injustice.* Christians believe that in the second tree God somehow was secretly subverting the ungodly politics of empires past and present.

While the first two trees are vitally important, it is really a third tree that captures my imagination in this sermon. The good news of the third tree speaks powerfully to those of us longing for a world of justice, peace, and social inclusiveness.

In Revelation 21-22, John poetically paints a portrait of a new heaven and a new earth. More specifically in Revelation 22:1, an angel takes John to the river of the water of life. This river in the New Jerusalem flows right down the middle of the street. The primary purpose of the river is to irrigate a tree. John calls it *the tree of life.* Permit me to talk about this tree of life for a moment.

First, the tree of life bears twelve kinds of fruit, and there is never an "off season." Every month, the tree produces an abundance of fruit. In other words, in God's new world, there is an abundance of what we need.

This is a remarkable word of hope in a world where an alarming number of children—especially black and brown children—are born in poverty and never have a chance to escape poverty.

In the ten years that have passed since September 11, 2001, we have heard much rhetoric about the immorality of terrorism. Certainly, there is no moral justification for the heinous violence that terrorists have enacted against our country and other countries. Yet by the same token, it is also immoral for the richest nation in the world to be so callous about the poverty of its own citizens and the citizens of the global community.

The tree of life, with its monthly yield of hunger-satisfying fruit, would have a hard time growing in our country and world. In our domineering quest for more money and better technology, we have contaminated the soil with toxic waste. More tragic than the *soil pollution*, however, is our *soul pollution*. Our souls have been polluted with the poisonous run-off of a mean-spirited capitalism that is more interested in the creation of profit than in the salvation of people. The only tree that matters to many in our world is the money tree whose green leaves have printed on them, ironically, "In God We Trust."

The tree that symbolizes God's future for the world is the tree of life. This tree teaches us that healing and hope will occur in this world when the vast majority of the world's resources are not consumed greedily by a small percentage of people who reside primarily in the United States. God's promise is that a day will come when abundance, not scarcity, will be the order of the day for all the world's inhabitants—and not just those with American passports. Many people are hurting and need healing, because in a land of plenty, a few have too much while so many cannot get enough to survive.

The miracle of the tree of life will ultimately be God's doing. Nevertheless, we are called right now to plant a seed for the tree of life to grow in this world. We are called to water that seed so that the tree of life might produce some fruit for impoverished people in the present even while we wait for God's future. I have met so many "religious" people who are waiting to go *up* to heaven. However, the book of Revelation teaches us that God is waiting on us to bring heaven *down* to earth through our loving sacrifice and courageous action. The tree of life has an abundance of fruit.

Also, according to John's vision, the tree of life is irrigated by the river of life that flows right down the middle of the street in the New Jerusalem.

In fact, the tree of life is actually not one tree, but at least two trees or maybe many trees. The river flows down the middle of the street, and on both sides of the river, the tree of life stands. There is a tree of life on the right side and a tree of life on the left side. In other words, God imagines a future for us where there will be unlimited and unrestricted access to privilege.

This is a mighty word of hope for people stuck in the old order, still riddled by networks of nepotism that favor the friends and cronies of a powerful elite, while denying access to necessary goods and services to whole segments of the world. In this nation, those who live on the right side of the tracks have state-of-the art schooling. Those who live on the wrong side are regularly enrolled in the school of hard knocks and missed opportunities. While we should gratefully acknowledge the grand strides our country has made, we also must acknowledge that America still perpetuates a subtle, sophisticated system of racial and economic apartheid.

Our world is characterized by unfair restrictions to privilege. But John declares that a future is coming when those ungodly restrictions will be removed. In the new city, the river sustaining the tree of life flows right down the middle of the street. There is a tree of life on the right side and a tree of life on the left side of the river. In God's glorious future, there will be no wrong side of the river; no wrong side of the tracks.

Everybody who has served God and embodied the truth of the gospel will have access to privilege. In God's future, there will be *no* sign on the tree of life that reads:

only whites allowed
only middle class allowed
only men allowed
only Christians allowed
only people with college degrees allowed
only heterosexuals allowed
only English-speakers allowed
only the young and able-bodied allowed
only the mentally well-adjusted allowed

When God's future is fully manifest, we will discover that many of the barriers that religious people have created do not represent God's inclusive intentions. The good news in Revelation 22 is the *promise of abundance* symbolized by the fruit of the tree of life and the *promise of access* symbolized by there being trees on both sides of the river.

There is one final feature of the tree of life that must be described. The tree has special leaves on it. Thanks be to God for the leaves on the tree of life! For the leaves of that tree are good for the healing of the nations. The final promise of the tree of life is the *promise of healing*.

Healing is what God's future will entail. God graciously allows us to get enough of heaven's healing now to make it through this troubled world. But our healing will not fully come until God's future has finally come. The full and final manifestation of God's future—some call it heaven—will be the time and place where our ultimate healing is granted. The longer I live, the more convinced I am that heaven will not be a classroom where our questions will be answered. It will be a hospital where our hurts will be healed.

None of us will sprint into eternity. All of us will limp into eternity, having been wounded by some tragedy, some disease, some disappointment, some miscalculation, some misstep. Thus, God will spend the first epoch of eternity simply applying healing balm to our hurting hearts.

The hope that keeps me struggling along is that someday we will be healed. Surely our world needs healing:

healing between women and men
healing between husbands and wives
healing between parents and children
healing among the races and religions
healing among the nations
healing among gays, lesbians, and heterosexuals
healing between conservatives and liberals
healing between red states and blue states
healing for persons infected with HIV-AIDS
healing for the entire world that has been affected by HIV-AIDS

Our ultimate healing will come in God's future, but I believe that we can reach up and grab a leaf on the tree of life right now. On behalf of a hurting world, you and I should reach up into the heavenly world and pull down one of those leaves and apply its healing balm:

Reach up: grab a leaf, and heal someone. The 1 billion people in our world lacking clean drinking water need you to grab a leaf on their behalf.

Reach up: grab a leaf, and heal someone. The 400 million people in our world infected with malaria need you to grab a leaf on their behalf.

Reach up: grab a leaf, and heal someone. More than 30 million people in our world living with HIV-AIDS need you to grab a leaf on their behalf.

Reach up: grab a leaf, and heal someone. The thousands of lonely children across this country need you to grab a leaf on their behalf before they turn to gangs and suicide.

The tree of life grows in another world, but through our faith, generosity, and advocacy, we can reach up to heaven, pull down a leaf, and heal somebody right here, right now. People of God, reach up . . . reach up . . . reach up . . . and then reach out. Amen.

The True Universal Health Care
Mark 10:46-52
Rev. Susan Sparks, senior minister, Madison Avenue Baptist Church, New York, New York, March 3, 2010.

The theologian Karl Barth said you should do theology with the Bible in one hand and the newspaper in the other. If you considered our Scripture this week in light of some of the newspaper headlines, especially that of the recent health-care debate, it takes on an entirely new light.

As Jesus and his disciples were leaving Jericho, Bartimaeus, a blind beggar, was sitting by the roadside. When he heard that it was Jesus of Nazareth, he began to shout out and say, "Jesus, Son of David, have mercy on me!" Several of the disciples went over and said, "Be quiet, and wait your turn. Can't you see there's a crowd waiting to see the Messiah?"

As Bartimaeus paused in silence, he felt a clipboard being thrust into his hands.

"Now," said John, one of the bossier of the disciples, "fill out the following thirteen forms. We need name, address, social security number, next of kin, and whether you have an HMO, PPO, or POS. Please indicate whether you have additional vision and/or dental coverage. Check the box on page five if this is a work-related injury. Fill out the duplicate form if you have any secondary insurance, read and sign the privacy statement at the end, and then return it to me with your insurance card."

Bartimaus paused, "I can't read . . . I'm blind."

"Well, then," said John in a huff, "just give me your insurance card, and we'll try to get you in the queue anyway."

Bartimaeus shook his head in shame, mumbling something under his breath.

"What did you say?" John demanded.

"I'm uninsured," Bartimaeus said quietly, his eyes averted.

"I still can't understand you!" blurted John.

"I AM UNINSURED!" yelled Bartimaeus.

A gasp came from the disciples. "Uninsured?!" they said, looking at each other with disgust . . . and the crowd began to back away from Bartimaeus.

"Do you have cash?" John demanded.

"No," said Bartemaeus.

"Do you have a credit card?"

"No."

"Do you have a job?"

"No."

"Well," John snapped, "you'll simply have to find another messiah."

Bartimaeus cried out even more loudly, "Son of David, have mercy on me!"

Jesus heard the man, stopped what he was doing, and said, "Who is that? Call him here."

And they called to the blind man, saying to him, "Take heart; get up, you've apparently been prequalified."

So throwing off his cloak, Bartimaeus sprang up and came to Jesus. Jesus said to him, "What do you want me to do for you?" Bartimaeus said to him, "My teacher, let me see again." Jesus said to him, "Go; your faith has made you well." Immediately, Bartimaeus regained his sight. And as he left, Jesus turned to the disciples and said, "Under no circumstances is this man to be charged a co-pay."

It makes you wonder if ole Bartimaeus would be able to get help today in 2011. As a blind beggar, I'm thinking No. There are *forty-six million* uninsured people in this country; a disproportionate number of whom are low-income and impoverished. No. I'm afraid ole Bartimaeus would be out of luck.

Yet over and over we are given the biblical mandate to care for the sick, care for the downtrodden, care for the poor.

Jeremiah 30:17 shows us that we have a God who heals: "Thus says the lord, I will restore you to health and heal your wounds."

Galatians 6:2 urges us to "carry each other's burdens, and in this way you will fulfill the law of Christ."

In Matthew 10:7, Jesus offers important directions to the disciples (and to us): "As ye go, proclaim the good news, heal the sick, cleanse the lepers . . . freely give as you have received."

And, of course, who could forget the story in Luke of the Good Samaritan. There, a man leaving Jerusalem was robbed and beaten, and no one, not the priest nor the Levite, would stop and help him. Then a Samaritan comes along who not only stops, but takes care of the man, dresses his wounds, and pays for his care. And what does Jesus says at end of story? He turns to his disciples and says, "*Go and do likewise.*"

Go and do likewise? Right.

Here we are, living in a country where people have to choose between food and medicine; where people are dying because they can't afford surgery.

This is a country where people can get insurance for their *pets* more readily than human beings! I'm not kidding. I looked up my own insurance company's website, and sure enough, there's a link for pets. It reads: "Your pet is part of the family. And like other family members, your pet has health needs. Pet insurance helps you manage the rising cost of treating your pet's illnesses and injuries. No pet is too old for coverage."

Yeah, I think there's a problem.

So what do we do about it? Well, I'm not sure anyone knows at this point. In fact, at this point, I think many of us wonder if we can do this at all? We're so bogged down in all the politics and maneuvering. You have to wonder, after all the years of talk and arguing and wrangling . . . is this even possible?

So many times in life, we get jaded and skeptical. We lose hope. Whether it is getting healthcare legislation through or simply finding a job, we lose hope because things just seem impossible. Yet anything is possible.

Let me share a story with you. A while back, I saw an AP news release from Duluth, Minnesota. The headline read, "Man is guilty of DWI in La-Z-Boy." The article goes on to explain that a Minnesota man pleaded guilt to riding his motorized La-Z-Boy chair while drunk. After leaving a local bar, he got in his chair and promptly crashed into a parked vehicle. Police said the chair was powered by a converted lawn-mower engine and had a stereo and cup holder. He was sentenced to six months of community service.

Yes, my friends, anything is possible in this world. Anything.

Even creating a healthcare plan . . . we know it is possible. The Canadians have done it, the UK has done it, the Scandinavians have done it.

But you know who else has put together a pretty good healthcare plan? One that we might seriously consider as a prototype for our own? God.

God has the best healthcare plan going. It covers everything: physical, mental, spiritual healing.

It's very affordable. In fact, it's free. There's not even a deductible.

There are no complicated forms or approval process. It's an "opt out" plan. You are given the plan at birth and keep it all your life, unless you yourself decide you don't want it (and even then you're still covered).

There are no preexisting conditions; it comes to you as you are, no matter how wounded or broken.

Most importantly, this plan is offered to *everyone*—from every walk of life—from every economic status—from every religion and culture.

This plan *is* the true universal healthcare plan. That's the one we should be working toward.

I can't solve the healthcare crisis in a fifteen-minute sermon. My message today is more about the lens, the paradigm, with which we approach this issue of caring for each other. When you take an issue out of your head, out of the intellectual side, and put it in your heart, the perspective changes.

This is not an issue involving statistics. This is an issue involving human beings. Like our friend Bartimaeus. This world is full of folks like Bartimaeus, people who, for no fault of their own, are unable to access basic rights and services in this country; human beings who are in pain.

The healthcare crisis in this country is not just some intellectual Rubik's Cube for us to chew on. It is an issue of the heart. It is an ethical mandate to—

Heal the sick

Bear each other's burden

Love our neighbor as ourself

When we overlay a biblical, ethical perspective on the problem, when we begin to see each other as God sees us, then that's the point we begin to transcend all the red tape, and greed, and politics, and fear, and move slowly but surely to the *true* universal healthcare that all God's children deserve.

Down by the River
Genesis 32:22-32

Dr. Thomas G. Long, professor of preaching, Candler School of Theology, Emory University, Atlanta. A version of this sermon appeared in the Pentecost 2009 issue of Journal for Preachers.

We should have known, shouldn't we, that it would have come to this. We should have known that we would find old Jacob out there, down by the riverbank, fighting as usual. We should have known that we would find Jacob in the darkness, sweating, wrestling, and brawling as always. It was in his nature, in his DNA.

Sometimes you can tell from the very beginning how a person will develop, what character will emerge. Years ago, when I was pastor of a church in Atlanta, I had in my congregation a family who had a troubled teenage daughter. She was having a hard time growing up. She is now, I'm happy to report, a mature and graceful woman and doing quite well. But in those days, she was struggling, always in trouble. She was in trouble at home, in trouble with teachers at school, occasionally in trouble with the police. After one of her scrapes with the law—it wasn't her first and it wouldn't be her last—her mother said to me in the midst of the turmoil, "I knew it would turn out this way. She was different from the other children from the day she was born. I knew when she was an infant that she was going to demand a lot of attention, that she was always going to be trouble."

Well, so it was with Jacob. One could see trouble coming from the day he was born. As a matter of fact, he was trouble even *before* he was born. In his mother's womb, the child that was to be Jacob was already brawling, fighting, and wrestling with his twin brother. You may remember that his mother Rebekah was not even sure she was going to be able to become pregnant. For a long time she thought she was infertile. She and her husband, Isaac, prayed desperately that she would become pregnant. Well, as they say, be careful what you pray for, because the result of Rebekah's prayer was that she ended up carrying twins, and one of them was a wrestler. Rebekah knew he was trouble even from the beginning. In fact he wrestled so vigorously with his twin brother and created such distress for Rebekah that she cried out in lament to God, "If this is what it means to be pregnant, I don't want it. As a matter of fact, if this is what it means to be pregnant, I'm not even sure I want to live." To put it mildly, Jacob was what we would today call a "problem pregnancy," but Rebekah pushed her way through it, and finally the two boys were born.

The first boy was born with a red complexion and hairy. They took one look at him and named him Esau. There is a little bit of a play on words here in the Hebrew, but his name means something like "red stuff." The second-born came out of the womb wrestling and fighting. In fact, he took hold of his brother Esau's foot and was trying to pull him back into the womb, to wrestle him back so that he could be born first, instead of Esau. His parents took one look at that act of aggression, ambition, and competition, and they named him Jacob, which means "the heel grabber," "the barroom brawler," the "wrestler," the "fighter."

P. T. Barnum once famously said that there is a sucker born every minute. Well, Jacob already knew that. In fact, there was a sucker born just the minute before he was, his twin brother Esau, and Jacob spent most of his childhood mastering the art of conning his slightly older brother. "Take a card, Esau, any card." By the time they were young men, Jacob had managed to weasel his brother's inheritance, to deceive their father, Isaac, and to wrestle away from his brother the blessing rightfully due him because he was the oldest. Jacob was a con artist extraordinaire. Soon he moved from trifling with his family of origin and onto richer territory. He pretended to be a naïve innocent to his future father in-law, Laban, and wound up at the end of the day with not only two of his daughters, but also with Laban's best livestock and most of his money. By the time we catch up with him in our story, Jacob is on the lam, running barely a step ahead of his creditors and his enemies.

In worship, we sometimes have prayers that begin, "O God of Abraham, Isaac, and Jacob." Do we really have any idea what we are saying, invoking Jacob's name over our prayers? This guy is a con artist, a flimflam man. He can steal the bullet out of your gun before you can shoot him. His whole life embodies what Woody Allen said to defend himself when he decided to have an affair with Mia Farrow's adopted

teenage daughter: "The heart wants what it wants." And when it wants
what it wants, it wrestles life and anything that gets in the way to the
ground in order to get it. We should have known it would have come to
this: old Jacob wrestling and fighting beside the river. It is in his DNA. It
is in his nature. Do we really know what we are saying when we pray to
the God of Jacob?

As a matter of fact, in the deepest part of our hearts, I think we *do*
know what we are saying when he pray in Jacob's name, because we recognize our own stories in his. Jacob is not just the man Jacob; he is Israel, the
people of God. And he is not just Israel; he is all of us, all human beings.
In our hearts, human beings are wrestlers and brawlers and fighters. That
is essentially what God told Rebekah when she complained about her
pregnancy. God said that it was not just two babies that were struggling in
Rebekah's womb. It was the divided human condition struggling there. It
was not just two babies; it was two nations. It was Israel and Edom,
hunters and gatherers, farmers and ranchers, red states and blue states, old
light and new light, liberals and conservatives. It's "Momma always liked
you better." "Yeah, but you were the apple of Daddy's eye." It is the human
struggle at war, and Jacob epitomizes it. And all of us are Jacob, because
our hearts want what they want, and we will wrestle life to the ground to
get it.

As biblical scholar Terry Fretheim once said of this story, "Well, there
is Jacob. Take him or leave him, and the astonishing thing about this story
is that God takes him." What God does is take Jacob the con man and
transform him into Jacob the human being. Jacob believes that he can
seize what he wants by the dint of his own strength. We see him swagger-
ing toward the promised land, boasting of his own strength, his fists
gnarled, ready to brawl his way forward. In fact, the only thing standing
between him and the promised land is the river Jabok and a mysterious
stranger. And this makes all the difference.

One day, after chapel at the seminary where I was teaching, I was
walking across campus, and one of my students hailed me, "Dr. Long, I
need a word with you."

I said, "I'm going to get a cup of coffee; do you want to join me?" And
she did. When we got our coffee, she said, "Here is what I want to talk to
you about. My supervising field education pastor is making me preach
next Sunday." Preaching professor that I am, I said, "Good." "No, it is not
good. He is making me preach the lectionary." Again, I said, "Good."

She said, "It is not good. Have you read the lectionary passages for next week? They are about judgment. I don't believe in judgment. I believe in love. I believe in mercy. I believe in kindness. It took me three years of therapy to get over judgment. I am not going to preach judgment."

We talked about that for a while, to no avail, and then she changed the subject. She wanted to tell me about her family. She and her husband were having a problem. It was their youngest son, the last to be at home. He was in trouble. He was giving them trouble. She said, "We don't even know his whereabouts most of the time. For example, last night my husband and I were having supper. We didn't know where my son was. We think he's involved with drugs. We just don't know where he is or what we're up against. All of a sudden, in the middle of supper, the door swings open and there he is. I said, 'Would you like some supper?' He looked like he was going to spit, stalked down the hall to his room, and slammed the door. My husband got up and turned on ESPN. That is what he does always in this situation. It is the way he always responds. But something got into me," she said. "I got up from the table and walked trembling down the hall. I am afraid of my own son, physically afraid of my own son. When I got to his room, I pushed open the door, and I said to him, 'Now you listen to me. I love you so much I am not going to put up with this anymore.'" I said to her, "I think you just preached a wonderful sermon on judgment."

That is what judgment is. It is not God punishing us; it is God setting things right. It is God saying to us, "I love you so much I am not going to put up with this anymore." The great theologian Karl Barth once said, "Do not fear the wrath of God; fear the love of God, for the love of God will strip away everything that stands between you and God."

There by the river Jabok, the love of God ambushed proud Jacob. There, down by the river, Jacob encountered the loving judgment of God. We don't know everything that happened there, but we do know what came out of it at the end. Jacob, the old street brawler, the old wrestler, got up changed and walked away with a limp. He got up transformed. He got up with a new name. He got up with a blessing to carry with him into the promised land.

I had a minor skirmish with the law recently. One day, after filling up my car with gas, I had to drive across four lanes of traffic to get into a left-hand turn lane. I darted across the lanes, but suddenly the light changed to red, the traffic stopped, and I found myself with the nose of my car in one lane and the tail of my car in another. I looked in the rearview mirror, and there were police lights behind me. The policeman got out and said, "Do you know what you did wrong?"

"No, I don't," I lied. He said, "You are impeding the flow of traffic." When you are a young man you get a ticket for speeding in a convertible. When you are my age, you get one for being in the way, impeding the flow of traffic. He wrote out the ticket and said to my question of what have I done wrong, "You have violated section 40-6-184 of the Georgia code."

"What is that?" I asked.

"You can look it up in any library," he said curtly, thrusting my citation through the window.

I am a Jacob-style wrestler. I was not going to take this sitting down. I went to the library, I looked it up, I read the language of the code, I did a text analysis on the specific language of the law, and I came to a firm conclusion: I did *not* impede the flow of traffic. Technically speaking, I was not impeding the flow of traffic, not according to the exact language of the law. So I went to the law school library, and I did a LexisNexis search on this section of the law. I got case law, I got background, I got definitions, and by the time my trial date came around, I had a file folder two inches thick that proved that I was innocent.

On the day of my trial, the judge called my name. "Would you please approach the bench." I picked up my file folder, flexing my Jacobean muscles, and walked up to the bench. The judge said, "The officer who arrested you is no longer employed by the county. There is no one here to bear witness against you. You are free to go." Something in me wanted to say, "Hey, you can't just dismiss my case like this! I have a file folder that says I'm innocent!" Suddenly I realized, Jacob that I am, I'd rather be right than free. I'd rather win the fight than be blessed by grace.

So down at the river Jabok, the mysterious stranger wrestles me, and wrestles you, to the ground. Who was the stranger? Was it divine? Was it human? Was it Jacob wrestling himself? Was it Esau? Was it Isaac? Old victims of his deceit returned in his imagination for revenge? Was it God? Was it all of the above? We don't know. All we do know is that when Jacob got through with the experience, he recognized that God was somewhere in it. "I have seen God face to face and I have lived and I have a blessing."

So look, if you are trying to find God. Don't just look in the Bethels, the shrines, and the sanctuaries. Look in the Jaboks, too. Don't just look in the mountain top experiences; look in the struggles as well. I think it is very important that the Christian life does not begin at Bethel. The Christian life does not begin with a magnificent anthem, or an inspiring sermon, or a moving worship service, or fantastic buildings with stained glass. The Christian life begins with baptism, where God says to all of us, "Okay, wrestler, I'll meet you down at the river." All we know is when we walk through the waters, we've got a limp, a new name, and a blessing.

I went to the grocery store the other day. I hate to grocery shop. It is one of my least favorite things to do. Causing me to be even more irritated was the fact that I ran into some people who were actually enjoying their grocery shopping. It was a mother and her young son, and they had learned how to make a game out of this. What they did was, she had a list and she would read the next item off the list, aluminum foil, paper towels. He knew exactly which brand she wanted. He would run around the store till he found it and come back bearing it like a trophy. She would applaud, smile, give him the next item on the list, and off he would go. You know how it is in the grocery store; you are going to meet people several times if you meet them once. About the fourth aisle over, it dawned on me: the little boy was mentally disabled. She caught me staring at them. "I was just admiring your relationship with your son," I said. "Yes," she said. "He is a blessing from God."

I don't know how many river Jaboks she has been through. All I know is she is on the other side of the water, standing in the promised land with a blessing from God.

You Are Stronger Than You Think
Judges 6:11-16
Rev. Dr. Pablo R. Diaz, vice-president, Guideposts outreach ministries.

One of the great tragedies of life is when a person with God-given potential misses out on the opportunities to make the most of their life and talents. Human beings have more power, more strength, and more capacity than they usually use in their lifetime. We have the inner resources: tremendous potential, enormous possibilities, and natural gifts to achieve greatness with our lives. Yet too many people never quite live up to it. We let our fears limit our possibilities. Our lack of faith undermines our potential. We think that the obstacle we face is greater than the God we serve.

There was once a sculptor who worked hard with hammer and chisel on a large block of marble. A little child who was watching him saw nothing more than large and small pieces of stone falling away left and right. He had no idea what was about to happen. A few weeks later when the child returned to the studio, he saw, to his surprise, a large, powerful lion sitting in the place where the marble had stood before.

With great excitement, the boy ran to the sculptor and said, "Sir, tell me, how did you know there was a lion in the marble?" "I knew there was a lion in the marble because before I saw the lion in the marble, I saw him in my own heart," the sculptor answered. "The secret is that it was the lion in my heart that recognized the lion in the marble" (Henri J. M. Houwen, Michael J. Christensen, and Rebecca J. Laird, *Spiritual Direction: Wisdom for the Long Walk of Faith* [San Francisco: Harpers, 2006] 16-17).

God is the master sculptor who gradually chips away until the lion in you is revealed . . . until the person you are destined to become is realized.

God sees in you all the resources that you need: tremendous potential and enormous possibilities.

God stretches you beyond your mental, physical, and spiritual limitations.

The greatest obstacle to what God sees and wants to do with you . . . is YOU.

In the book of Judges, one of the characters is Gideon. He was chosen by God in a time of crisis to act boldly and courageously on behalf of Jehovah's community. God sends an angel to visit Gideon, an ordinary farmer, living in a time when Israel had no kings but only local heroes who God raised to lead their communities against powerful military powers. The Israelites had forsaken the ways of the Lord, and for seven years had been subjected to the oppression of the Midanities, who ruined their crops, invaded their land, and impoverished their people.

The desperate nature of the situation was illustrated by Gideon's threshing his wheat, not as customarily done with oxen on an open hilltop, but by hand in the cramped quarters and secrecy of a wine press. The angel sits under an oak tree where Gideon is threshing wheat in a wine press. He is hiding in fear from those who will come and steal his crop. The angel says to Gideon, "The Lord is with you, mighty warrior." God sees Gideon as a mighty warrior, not as a frightened farmer. God sees Gideon as stronger than he thinks he is and more capable than he imagined himself to be.

Gideon's dialogue with the angel reveals his beliefs, assumptions, and self-perception. Like others before and after him, he offers reasons for his inability to carry out the mission. Moses felt insecure and uncertain about his capacity to fulfill the mission. Jeremiah felt inadequate and not qualified to bring the message of God to the people. Jeremiah tells God, "I do not know how to speak; I am too young." But the Lord said to me, "Do not say, 'I am too young.' You must go to everyone I send you to and say whatever I command you." (Jer 1:6-7)

Retired Major General (and former chief of chaplains for the United States Army) Gaylord Taylor Gunhus would remind his chaplains, "God doesn't call the equipped. He equips those he calls." *God will raise you up to be more than you can be; therefore, you are capable.*

A first-year student in seminary informed the professor that she would once again not have her paper in on time. He said to her, "You are going to be a pastor. Pastors must be punctual. You cannot stand up on Sunday and say, 'I had hoped to have a sermon for you today, but first one thing and then another came up. We are going to break up into small groups instead of listening to me preach today.'"

She responded, "I agree with you. I have few obvious gifts for ministry. I'm always late. I'm too old. I know I have no business being in seminary. I have told God that repeatedly. My being here is God's idea, not mine." Upon reflection, the professor realized the student had it right. We are in ministry, in service to God and God's world, because we have been called and put here by God, who loves to make something out of nothing.

The next time you feel like God can't raise you up to be more than you can be, just remember: Noah had problems with alcohol. Abraham and Sarah were too old. Isaac was a daydreamer. Jacob was a liar. Joseph was abused and falsely imprisoned. Moses had a stuttering problem. Samson was a womanizer. Rahab was a prostitute. David had an affair and was a murderer. Elijah was suicidal. Isaiah preached naked. Jonah ran from God. Naomi was a widow. Job went bankrupt. Peter denied Christ. Martha worried about everything. Zaccheus was too small. Paul was too religious. Timothy was too young. And Lazarus was dead. Now: no more excuses! God can use you to your full potential.

Gideon doesn't see himself as a mighty warrior. Instead, he focuses on the circumstances that the people of God are facing. He tells the angel, "Why has all this happened to us?" Why are the Midianites messing with our food and land? But the Lord tells him to "go in the strength you have and save Israel out of Midian's hand, and am I not sending you?" *God's strength is within you; therefore, you are powerful.*

In the midst of great difficulty lies the greatest potential for ordinary individuals to release their greatest talent. The great Roman thinker Horace said, "Difficulties elicit talents that in more fortunate circumstances would lie dormant."

Where is the strength coming from? God's presence, power, word, and might within and outside of Gideon. Gideon's inner power comes from God. As Jesus said, "The kingdom of God is within you."

Still, the story says, Gideon continues to resist the message of the angel and the call of God to deliver the people from the Midianites. He tells the angel, "How can I save Israel? My clan and family is the weakest of my tribe, and I am the least in my family." And God answers Gideon, "I will be with you." If God is on your side, you are stronger than you think. *God turns your weaknesses into strength; therefore, you are strong.*

The Apostle Paul (who knew firsthand about personal struggle and ministry hardships) discovered that God turns his weaknesses into strength. In 2 Corinthians 12:10 he states, "For when I am weak, then I am strong."

In Hebrews 11:32-34, the author names champions of the faith who faced adversity yet fulfilled their mission with God's presence and power on their side.

"And what more shall I say? I do not have time to tell about Gideon, Barak, Samson, Jephthah, David, Samuel and the prophets, who through faith conquered kingdoms, administered justice, and gained what was promised; who shut the mouths of lions, quenched the fury of the flames, and escaped the edge of the sword; whose weakness was turned into strength, and who became powerful in battle and routed foreign armies."

English mystic Evelyn Underhill said, "God's power is brought into action just where our power fails."

When you believe and visualize the mighty warrior within you, you can and will do incredible things, accomplish the unexpected, and attain your goals. Dr. Norman Vincent Peale said, "Think yourself strong." When you place yourself in the hands of God, the master sculptor, there is not a mission, task, or assignment given to you by the Almighty that is too great for you to fulfill—because it all depends on whose hands it's in.

It Depends Whose Hands It's In!

A basketball in my hands is worth $19. A basketball in LeBron James's hands is worth about $20 million. It depends whose hands it's in.

A baseball in my hands is worth about $6. A baseball in Alex Rodriguez's hands is worth $25 million. It depends whose hands it's in.

A golf club in my hands is useless. A golf club in Tiger Woods's hands is a PGA Championship. It depends whose hands it's in.

A rod in my hands will keep away a wild animal. A rod in Moses' hands will part the mighty sea.

A slingshot in my hands is a kid's toy. A slingshot in David's hands is a mighty weapon.

Two fish and five loaves of bread in my hands is a couple of fish sandwiches. Two fish and five loaves of bread in Jesus' hands will feed thousands.

Nails in my hands might produce a birdhouse. Nails in Jesus Christ's hands will produce salvation for the entire world. It depends whose hands it's in.

In God's hands, you are stronger than you think!

Skinny-Dip Sermon
John 21:1-17

Dr. Anna Carter Florence, professor of homiletics, Columbia Theological Seminary, Decatur, Georgia. She preached this sermon at the Festival of Homiletics, Minneapolis, Minnesota, 17 May 2011.

When Simon Peter heard that it was the Lord, he put on some clothes, for he was naked, and jumped into the lake.

I've been taking a close look at Peter lately. I'm sure the man grew into a lovely apostle and a first-rate leader of the emergent church in Palestine, but from a teacher's perspective, let me tell you: he is not the easiest disciple to have in class. I get one or two Simon Peters every year. I get one or two Nathaniels, and Thomases, and Marthas, and Marys, for that matter; they all show up at seminary, eventually. The whole biblical cast. And they all lean on the same verbs as their predecessors: the Nathaniels complain that nothing good can come out of Galilee, the Thomases doubt everything on principal, the Marys sit at Jesus' feet in the library with their Hebrew flash cards, and the Marthas run for student council president. And I really do enjoy them all, with the possible exception of the ones who are auditioning for the role of the Disciple Whom Jesus Loved—because reclining on Jesus' breast isn't the only requirement for preaching. But it's the Peters who stretch me most, as a teacher. Peter has the verbs that test my patience, and maybe yours.

When Simon Peter heard that it was the Lord, he put on some clothes, for he was naked, and jumped into the lake.

Here is what I have noticed about Peter. Whenever he shows up in the text, he changes the subject from Jesus to himself.

Walking on water? Hey, let me try that!

Transfiguration? Let me build three shelters, one for each of you!

Jesus arrested? Well, I'm packing a sword and I'm gonna cut off your ear!

It changes the subject and slows down the action. Because now Jesus has to intervene, so Peter doesn't drown or die of embarrassment or the sword. This is what happens when you have socially awkward disciples, who have something to prove. I've seen it in the text. I've seen it in the classroom. You've seen it in your churches! Whenever Peter shows up, there's a script you have to play out with him, because he doesn't believe, yet, that Jesus really loves him exactly for the rock he is. He thinks he has to be the best at every facet of discipleship: "Though all become deserters because of you, I will never desert you! I am ready to go with you to prison and to death!" Which, of course, he can't. Not at this stage, anyway. Not while he has something to prove and a lot to hide.

When Simon Peter heard that it was the Lord, he put on some clothes, for he was naked, and jumped into the lake.

It's such a Peter thing to do: get dressed and then jump in the water. None of the other disciples do it. They know someone has to row the boat ashore, help to trim the sail, drag the net of fish; it takes a lot of people working together when you've got a big catch. When Jesus said, "Leave your nets and follow me," he didn't mean, "Leave them for someone else to haul in so *you* can get to me first!" The other disciples know this. They think like a group. Peter thinks like a lone ranger. He's all "I" statements: *I'm going fishing. I'm jumping overboard. You guys can do what you want.* If one of your disciples is always changing the subject and turning your ministry into a competition, it slows down the action.

Maybe that's why I've thought so much about this weird little verse about jumping into the lake with all his clothes on. Let me put it this way: if you want to swim fast, you don't stop to put on your jeans and a sweatshirt. The less you have on to slow you down, the better, which is why racing swimmers even shave their arms and legs. So if Peter was already "stripped for work," as the RSV puts it, why not just stay that way? Skinny-dip, as it were; wear your birthday suit. Jump in, swim fast, be the first one to give Jesus a big, wet, awkward hug, and get dressed later. That's what I'd expect from Peter, given his usual verbs. Not what we have in the text.

You know what I love about human beings? Our actions always betray us. They show us what's really going on, underneath all the words. Just like our sermons. There is nothing like preaching a text to strip you naked.

It was one of my students, named Lucy, who recently reminded me of this. A bunch of us were sitting around talking about this passage after class one day, going through it verse by verse, and I was asking them what they thought about it. And Lucy said, "You know what I hear in this passage? Genesis 3. Their eyes were opened and they knew that they were naked, and they covered themselves, and hid from God."

Well. I realized that I'd been looking in the wrong direction. Peter doesn't put on some clothes because he's an awkward, compulsive, competitive dork. He puts on some clothes because he is *naked before the Lord!* And sometimes, that is the *last* thing you want to be.

If I am naked before the Lord, then I have to really look at myself. I have to really look at myself as a preacher. What I see and what I don't see. What I say and what I don't say. All the times I changed the subject from God to myself, because I wanted the congregation to notice me, and like me, and think I'm wonderful. All the times I thought I should be able to walk on water by preaching the perfect sermon, if I only had enough faith. All the times I thought Jesus needed me to defend him by slicing a sword through my listeners. All the times I denied him, and there were a lot more than three. If I'm naked before the Lord, I have to look at all that, and it can be unbearable. I'd rather go fishing. I'd rather put on all my clothes and jump in the lake. Oh, to be a preacher is to swim with a lot of wet, heavy stuff dragging you down. And it's hard to take it off.

So here's what Jesus does. He waits for us on the beach. He lets us try to swim *our* way, with all our wet, heavy stuff, and then he gives us a chance to get rid of it. It's not quick. It's not easy. This is Jesus, after all; he's not into cheap grace. But he does show us that we can choose some new verbs.

It starts with a charcoal fire and three questions. Jesus gives the disciples breakfast and then asks Peter, "Simon, son of John, do you love me?" The last time someone asked Peter three questions, he didn't answer them so well. It was the night Jesus was arrested: various strangers asked Peter if he knew Jesus, if he was one of his followers. Peter said no. Three times. Like Jesus said he would. On the beach, Jesus reframes the questions. He doesn't ask Peter if he *knows* him. He asks Peter if he *loves* him. That's the verb that really counts. And this time, Peter says yes.

I know you've preached this dozens of times. I've *heard* it dozens of times, since this text is a seminarian favorite. But do you know what I've never noticed, in all those readings? I've never noticed the charcoal fire. And I probably wouldn't have, if I hadn't been thinking about a wet, soggy Peter.

What's the first thing you do when you get out of the water? You try to get warm. You dry off, if you've brought a towel, and you put on dry clothes. That's important, if it's cold. You don't want to catch a chill, and you don't want to invite hypothermia, so rule number one is you get dry. And if you don't happen to have beach towels, a charcoal fire will do very nicely.

Of course, you *can* cook breakfast over a fire; if you're hungry, that would probably be the first thing that would come to mind. But if you've just jumped into the sea with all your clothes on and you're wet and cold, you're not thinking about *food.* You're thinking about *getting warm,* and a charcoal fire is a godsend! You stand with your back to it, inching as close as you can without getting burned. You stretch out your hands over the flames. You take your wet clothes and hang them up, so the heat will dry them—as Peter knows very well.

Think: when was the *last* time Peter sat around a charcoal fire?! Right. And here's Jesus, ready with another one. Maybe he knows Peter needs a big ritual in order to cleanse that memory, or maybe he knows Peter needs a big reminder of what can happen to a disciple who only deals in the first-person singular. Whatever the reason, Jesus doesn't just give Peter a chance to answer three questions correctly; *he recreates the scene!* He makes Peter remember his verbs, how he sat around that other charcoal fire the night of Jesus' arrest, "warming himself." That's how the text puts it: "warming himself." And how naked can Peter be, but to put on his clothes, jump in the lake, swim to shore, and find a *charcoal fire* waiting for him, with all the history and baggage *that* implies?! How nakedly predictable can we be, but to walk straight into a scene Jesus recreates just for us?!

Oh, the exquisite agony of it: the night of your worst nakedness, replayed for all to witness! And because *you* were the one who jumped into the sea and got wet in the first place, *you're* the only one who needs to "warm yourself" by the charcoal fire. You're the only one who will have to relive that terrible verb.

"Warming yourself." It's a verb you need when you're wet and cold, but it doesn't work so well in other contexts. It's what Peter was reduced to, the night Jesus was arrested: warming himself around a charcoal fire. One verb led to another, and before he knew it, he took up "deny" and followed.

"Warming yourself." It's a real changing-the-subject verb. Jesus is being interrogated in the next room, and you're sitting by a charcoal fire. Life-and-death stuff is happening right outside the church doors, and we're singing camp songs around a cozy fire. Doesn't preaching feel like that sometimes? Doesn't *church* feel like that—the ultimate place to warm yourself in a cold, wet world?! And how tempting it is to stand around *that* fire, where everything gospel is toasty warm! Sermons that feel good and get your blood moving and don't cost you anything, because you can always bow out when you have to. You can always say, "No, I'm not one of *those* followers." You can always keep silent.

Unless it's Jesus who makes the charcoal fire for you instead, and gives you a different verb. He doesn't invite you to come and warm yourself. He says, "Come and have breakfast. And bring some of the fish that you just caught."

What would it be like, to let go of all those former things? To be a preacher who knows that her eyes are opened and she isn't ashamed of what she sees? To be a preacher who knows that he is naked before the Lord because he is *known*? We can choose that. We can choose it whenever we want. The nourishment of bread over the weight of heavy, heavy coverings. The fire of discipleship over easy warmth. The freedom of skinny-dipping in the text because we don't need to put on any fig leaves; there isn't anything in God's word that we can't look at. And there isn't anything we have to hide from, either. Because *there is nothing that can separate us from the love of God in Christ Jesus our Lord*—and *that*, you have to preach.

You know, when I think about it, every one of my students is Peter. We *all* are. Putting on clothes and jumping in and walking smack into whatever life-transforming verbs Jesus has planted on the set for us. I admit it would be nice if I could keep my seminarian Peters from packing their swords in class, but that will come in time; I know it will. They'll graduate, and go out into the church, and meet *you*, and you'll help them figure it out.

"Come and have breakfast," Jesus tells Peter, "and bring some of the fish that you just caught for us to eat together, over a charcoal fire." He tells us, too. And then he tells us to go and feed his sheep—no, wait: *his lambs*. First, it's the lambs. You know who the lambs are, right? They're the ones who wandered away and got lost, trying to warm themselves; *you* remember. That's why you'll be so good at seeking them out. You know what kind of charcoal fire cooks our bread.

Amen.

Attitude Changes Altitude
John 5:1-18

Dr. Mark Craig, senior minister, Highland Park United Methodist Church, Dallas; baccalaureate address at Southern Methodist University, May 13, 2011.

Bobby Spencer was a West Virginia coal miner who, about seven years ago, was a couple of hundred feet below the earth with his colleagues when the shaft he was in totally collapsed. After the dust had settled, Bobby Spencer knew that he was trapped. Intuitively, he knew that he was alone. He surmised that some of his buddies had died and that some had scurried out and were safe.

On the ground above the mine they tried to figure out if there was any life down below. They ran mechanical devices down but found no signs of life. After a while they gave up hope, assuming everyone had died. Bobby Spencer felt differently.

He was trapped and alone, but he was very much alive. He decided that he would start doing what he did best. He dug. He dug, and dug, and dug. With his hands, bloodied hands, he started clawing one rock at a time. In his own words, he said there was only one thing he was saying to himself. It was a Scripture verse he had learned in Sunday school in West

Virginia. He thought Paul had said it. Those words he kept repeating were these: "I can do all things through Christ who strengthens me."

"I can do all things through Christ who strengthens me . . . I can do all things through Christ who strengthens me." He kept digging, and digging, and digging until he saw the light. This is an amazing story! He kept digging, and digging, and digging until he saw the light.

His attitude literally determined his altitude. He kept going up because he believed he was being strengthened by the power that was greater than himself.

I was reading not long ago about 200 CEOs who were asked a very simple question: "What one characteristic creates success for leadership in the nation's largest corporations in America?" Eighty percent of them answered "attitude." An attitude of enthusiasm is the most important thing of all. That was the characteristic. Not brainpower! Not salesmanship and ingenuity! But an attitude of enthusiasm was their response.

Today it is just the opposite with this fellow in our Scripture lesson, who is trapped (or apparently trapped) and can't move (or refuses to move) after thirty-eight years. I think it is "refuses to move." Thirty-eight years! This is a depressing story. Thirty-eight years sitting by this pool. The Bible says he is paralyzed. But that is suspect, because when Jesus says, "Do you want to walk?" he doesn't even answer the question after thirty-eight years of not walking! Instead, he starts blaming people about why he has been stuck so long in his life. Stuck for thirty-eight years beside this pool with a cast of characters that hardly ever changes, and nothing good happens in his life until Jesus Christ gives him an ultimatum to "GET UP AND WALK!" Do something with your life! And that required a change in attitude. Up to this time, there were two songs that he had been singing. One refrain is simply this: "No one is helping. Everybody's doing this or that which hurts me." He was blaming everything on everyone. He wouldn't take any responsibility for his own life. And the second thing is implicit, and maybe it is just because I don't like the guy much that I say this, but it is implicit: The second refrain is that he starts enjoying his own misery. I mean, when given the chance to change his life, he changes the subject. He starts enjoying his own misery and likes hearing the sound of his own complaining. Do you know anyone like that? Who starts to like their own misery?

So Jesus challenges him.

When my son was a senior in high school and playing basketball, if a kid could jump, they would say, "Man, he's got ups." "He's got ups." And I remember if the kid could really jump, they'd say, "He's got amazing ups." In the little school where my son was, occasionally (not often) a young man would come along who could really jump, who could jump out of the gym. Almost with reverence, he would get the ultimate compliment: "See him? He's got serious ups!" Since when I played I had no ups, when someone had serious ups, he got my attention. Jesus got the attention of the man by the pool by offering some serious ups. Seven serious ups. If you're at all interested in your altitude, meaning your success in life, he gives seven serious ups for improving your attitude to leverage your altitude. And they are these:

Wake up, listen up, 'fess up, look up, get up, step up, and don't give up!

For just a minute, let me look at these seven suggestions with you, these seven ups.

I went to the hospital yesterday to visit a church member who is a good friend. He had been admitted to Presbyterian Hospital with a stroke. I went into his room, and we talked. His wife called it a "moderate stroke." I don't like that language. To me, if it's a stroke, it's a stroke. I sat down, and we talked. He had driven fifteen miles from work to the hospital instead of calling 911. I thought I'd give him a lecture about that. Instead, I said, "I'm sorry. I'm praying for you. I never thought you'd be here." And he was gracious, but in a little way kind of brushed it off. He always tries to be a man's man. He said to me, "You know, this was probably a good wake-up call." I just nodded my head, but down deep I was asking myself the question, "What is the difference between a good wake-up call and a bad one?" I mean, the truth is, if you don't get the wake-up call, you've missed something pretty important. Wake-up calls are important, and so they're all good, usually. You don't like hearing them, but they keep you from missing something crucial.

Jesus looks at a man who had been paralyzed for thirty-years and gives him a wake-up call. "You're wasting your life! Do you want to get up and do something with it or not? This is your wake-up call." That's a serious UP. *Wake up!*

The second thing Jesus says is, "*Listen up!*" Listen up, meaning, "I've got something very important to tell you about your life."

Every coach I had in junior and senior high school used that phrase. After practice, they'd get everybody together and always say the same thing. First, you take one knee. You never dare take two knees. You don't sit on your helmet or your bottom. You don't stand up. The coach always says the same thing. I don't know why it's so important, but you always take one knee. Then the coach always says, "Listen up!" "Listen up." He wouldn't scream it at you. Coaches scream a lot, but he wouldn't scream that. He'd say it really slow and with a mellow voice, and everybody would get in real close. "Listen up." And then he'd tell us that we could win the game. We were good enough. We were better than we thought. We can win the game. We can win it. And, of course everybody loves hearing that because we all want to be told, if we only listen up, that we're better than we think we are. We all want to hear that we really can be winners. That is all that Jesus says to the man at the pool. "Wake up. And listen up. You can be better than you are, languishing here for thirty-eight years." I mean, that's real simple.

I was at a conference at the Crystal Cathedral twenty-five years ago (when Robert Schuller was in his prime). There were about twenty of us who participated. A woman leading the workshop took a huge white sheet of paper and taped it to the wall. She took a black Marks-A-Lot out of her pocket and put one dot, not two, one dot right in the middle of the paper. She asked a fellow who was in the group, "What do you see?" He said, "I see a black dot." She then did something I thought was boring. She went around to all twenty of us and asked, "What do you see? What do you see?" And all of us answered, "Black dot, black dot, black dot, black dot." Then after everyone says "black dot," she said, "I agree with you. I see a black dot, but that is not what I want to talk about today. I want to talk about all this white space that none of you mentioned. None of you acknowledged it, and none of you seem to appreciate it. I want to talk about this because this is your life. This is your life, and you miss it. You don't acknowledge it. You don't appreciate it. And I want to talk to you this morning so you can maximize it." I thought it was a great illustration of what is being said when Jesus says to that man, "Listen up!" I want to talk to you about all this space in your life that you can fill up with good things. So he says, "Wake up. Listen up."

And real quick, he says *"Fess up,"* as in "confess." Because we haven't lived our lives like we've wanted to live our lives, and we've gotten in some trouble. You've got to confess what you've done or failed to do if you want to be more and do better.

The fourth serious up is *"Look up!"* "God, I need your help. I admit I've had some problems. I need your help. And I am aware that I cannot lift myself up on my own power. I need power only You can provide."

The fifth is *"Get up!"* This is interesting to the man. As compassionate as Jesus is, you would think he'd give the man a hand, but he doesn't do anything. He just says, "Get up," and walks off . . . only to walk back a little later to see if the man has gotten up or not. Essentially he's saying, "I've done everything that I can do. It's up to you now." After you confess and ask God to help you, you've got to do something on your own. You've got to get up.

And, of course, the sixth is *"Step up!"* You've got to take the first step. In baseball, you've got to step up to the plate. If you don't step up to the plate, you can't swing. If you don't swing, you can't hit the ball. If you don't hit the ball, you can't get around to home plate. If you don't get around to home plate, you can't win. I mean, it is as simple as that. You have to step up.

And when you step up to the plate, you don't worry about swinging, you don't worry about striking out. That is the seventh point: *"Don't give up!"* We all strike out. We all swing and miss and swing and miss and feel like giving up. But Jesus says to the man, "After thirty-eight years, you've just about given up. Don't do that! You never win if you give up."

One of our ministers told an amazing story the other day. We were in our staff meeting, sitting in a big circle, and we were all invited at the beginning to share joys and concerns. Things that have happened in your life that are good, we can celebrate. Problems or troubling issues in your life, we can pray for. So one of our ministers says, "I'm not sure if this is a joy or concern. It is kind of a combo . . . a joy/concern." Everyone asked what it was, and she said, "It is about my cousin. He is forty-eight years old and has been a bachelor all his life. We've always wanted him to get married, but he never has. Never found the right person." Forty-eight years old, and they'd kind of given up on him. But hear the rest of the story. He was in O'Hare Airport a few months ago, and he got bumped. He was on an overbooked flight. Usually when that happens you are not on the plane yet, and they ask if anybody wants to get a free voucher. They promise you a room at the Four Seasons but end up putting you up at the Motel 8. But this was different. I've never heard of this before. I don't know exactly how it happened, but he was bumped after he was already on the plane. They had a hundred and thirty seats, and somehow there were a hundred and thirty-two people inside the plane. So they had to bump two who had already gotten onto the plane, and his number was called. He and one other person. They didn't offer to pay him anything. It was too late. They didn't offer to put him up, and there weren't any flights out. So he is standing there at the ticket counter with this one other person, who had also been bumped. I would have had flames coming out my ears at that point, but he was just standing there calmly. And he looks to his right at this woman about his age, the other person who had been bumped, and instead of going nuts he says to her, "Would you like to have dinner, and we can commiserate getting bumped?" She said Yes. Two and a half months later, they were married. When you get bumped (and who doesn't get bumped from time to time in life?), you can get bitter or you can get better. He gets better. In fact, he gets a lot better. He gets a wife. At the counter. If he hadn't been bumped, he wouldn't have found the love of his life. It's a great story. Don't give up!

Those are the seven ups.

I was at the SMU Baccalaureate ten days ago. It was an honor for me to be asked to speak in that immense auditorium. It is huge. You have those multi-balconies, and all the parents are up above in two upper balconies. Eighty percent parents, and twenty percent kids. Clearly the kids aren't excited about being there, and I'm thinking, "Oh, this is going to be a tough speech. Who am I giving this for? Is it for the parents or the kids?" I decide, "I'm going to speak to the kids." But I look out and start getting scared, because I realized that ninety-five percent of these kids graduating from Southern Methodist University are smarter than I am. There is an average SAT of 1300. So I'm sitting there thinking, "What do I have to say to them?" Then another onslaught of fear came over me because I know for a fact that four of those students had perfect SAT scores. They scored 1600. You say, "What does that mean?" Let me tell you what it means. It means 100 percent of the time they can tell you when this train leaving this station going sixty miles per hour and that train leaving that station going a hundred miles an hour will meet. That's what that means. One hundred percent of the time, they're right. And I'm thinking, "Gee, I don't have anything to say to them." And then I thought about this sermon coming up and decided, what the heck! I'll just tell these kids the most important thing in this country they need to know about success. *Your attitude will determine your altitude.* And I thought of Bobby Spencer being trapped and clawing his way back to the top. We're all trapped from time to time. Who isn't trapped? Who isn't bumped? Attitude, if it isn't everything, is 95 percent of the ballgame. So I told them that. I said what you feel in your heart is much more important that what you think in your head. That's just the deal.

The second thing I said to them was, "Some of you, particularly you kids who know how to get these trains to meet at a certain place, are going to get PhDs. But, some of you who set out to get PhDs will do all your coursework and then be tempted not to do your dissertation. That's called getting an ABD, an "All But Dissertation," and that's not a degree. Don't do that. Don't quit. Don't give up before you reach your goal. And the way to get the PhD instead of the ABD is simply a matter of attitude. If you stop short of your goal, maybe it's because you already have a kind of an ABD. It's called "All But Desire." I told them that is a truly crucial word in their lives: the *desire* to have the attitude to reach the altitude that you want to achieve in your life. I said Jesus can help you. He gives you seven serious ups. Seven serious ups that can drive your attitude—but these ups are irrelevant if you don't have the desire. That's what Jesus was getting at when he asked the man at the pool, "Do you want to be healed?" If you have the desire, then Jesus gives you the tools—the seven ups for success: wake up, listen up, 'fess up, look up, get up, step up, and when you're bumped, don't give up.

Can God Find Us?
Matthew 2:1-12

> *Michael B. Brown, senior minister, Marble Collegiate Church, New York, New York.*

While standing on the subway platform waiting for the 6 Train, I overheard two women chatting. It was a busy December day. The platform was crowded, and we strangers stood shoulder-to-shoulder. So I couldn't help but overhear when one said to the other, "There's not much holiday cheer in our house this Christmas. My husband still can't find work, and we're going through our savings at an alarming rate." Her friend, trying to be cheerful, answered, "Well, I'll bet Santa will still find your apartment," to

which the first woman replied, "I'm not sure even God can find our apartment!"

Some of us know the feeling. Whether you are living through financial
crisis, illness, grief, relational difficulties, or any of a thousand other
sources of stress, sometimes it's easy to suspect that even God has lost sight
of us.

It is understandable that the Magi had a tough time locating Jesus. To
their credit, they got close. When some of us were in Bethlehem last
spring, a member of our party said, "I always imagined these two cities
were miles and miles apart. But Bethlehem and Jerusalem are like one city
simply separated by this awful wall." The Magi got close. If you make it to
Jerusalem, you've almost made it to Bethlehem.

And to be honest, why wouldn't they have stopped in Jerusalem? If
they were looking for a king, Jerusalem was the place to look. The king of
the Jews would obviously be in Jerusalem. I would have gone there, too.
Even if the star went on to Bethlehem, I doubt that I would have.
Bethlehem? Little, out of the way Bethlehem? A village whose name means
"house of bread"? I'm supposed to find a messiah in a bakery? I don't think
so. Let's go to the city where the king dwells. Let's go to Jerusalem.

Years ago I had a colleague who spent most of her life in love with one
man. He and she had been best friends since grade school, but for her it
was much deeper than friendship. She was a beautiful woman in every
way—spiritually, physically, and in her personality. Her friend used to call
her "the total package" and said whoever married her would be a lucky
man. But she did not want "whoever." She wanted him. Meanwhile he
went through a series of three marriages, each of which failed. He would
come to his friend with fears and tears each time a marriage began to
unravel, and she would encourage and comfort him. She always remained
entirely proper and usually urged him to try and salvage the marriage. One
day she walked into my office and spilled out the whole story. At one point
she said, "He has spent so many years looking for love that he isn't able to
find that standing right in front of him is love. He isn't willing to see." The
Magi knew what they wanted to find, but looked in the wrong place. The
star went on another five miles, but they were not willing to see.

Herod greeted those Wise Men with wise men of his own. Herod, as
you know, was a paranoid of the first degree, even murdering family members whom he considered a threat. Thus, he received the news of a new
king with alarm . . . until, that is, he called his own wise men into the

room. "Tell me," said Herod, "where is this child who is born to be king of the Jews?" And they answered, "In Bethlehem in Judea, for this is what the prophet has written: 'But you, Bethlehem, small in the land of Judah, are by no means least among the rulers of Judah; for out of you will come a ruler who will shepherd my people Israel.'" Out of Bethlehem? The bakery? Herod must have felt like laughing. And so apparently he became dismissive. He basically said to the Magi, "Go to Bethlehem. If you find anything, let me know." Had Herod thought there was anything significant to find, he would have made that short five-mile trip himself, with soldiers in tow. But, as Nathanael implied a few years later, nothing good was expected to come out of Bethlehem, "small in the land of Judah." The Magi couldn't even find the place. It was the home of a handful of breadmakers and late-night shepherds who would have echoed the sentiments of a woman waiting for the 6 Train: "I'm not sure even God can find our apartment!"

So what about us? We may reside in New York City, but how many of us actually live in our own version of Bethlehem? The star shines over the rest of Manhattan with all its glitter and glory, but we suspect even God can't find our apartment.

"I audition for every part, but someone younger or prettier or with a better agent always gets the role."

"I write diligently and creatively, but someone who has to use a ghost writer gets published."

"My voice is as strong as anyone's, but I wait tables while teenaged rock stars who can't hit a note above middle C play in Madison Square Garden."

"I have a strong resumé. But I cannot find work, and it is demoralizing to see my neighbors rush out each morning to go to their jobs while I sit home, waiting for a phone call that doesn't come."

"My child is on drugs."

"My husband is unfaithful."

"My mother is dying."

"I feel abandoned and afraid and wonder if even God can find me."

So often, our experience is Bethlehem, close to the seat of joy and power, but not quite in it. But then comes the Christmas story: "After Jesus was born in Bethlehem in Judea, during the time of King Herod, Magi from the east came to Jerusalem." So what if the Magi came to Jerusalem! God incarnate came to Bethlehem! That's the Christmas message. That is the Christian message. "After Jesus was born in Bethlehem of Judea . . ."

I love the story of the six-year-old whose mother asked him to sweep the back steps of their home. Company was coming over in an hour, and she wanted everything to be neat. "But Mom," he replied, "it's dark out. I'm scared of the dark." "Son," she answered firmly, "I have a million things to do, and I want you to help me. I'm just asking one thing. Go out there, and sweep the porch." He protested: "Mom, I'm afraid to be alone in the dark." "You're not alone," she said, appealing to his lessons from Sunday school. "Jesus is out there with you." The child pondered that for a second, then opened the back door just enough to stick a broom through it, and before shutting it, whispered, "Jesus, since you're out there anyway, would you mind sweeping the porch for me?"

Jesus is "out there," in the cold, in the shadows, in the dark nights of the soul, in the scary places, in our Bethlehem, with us and for us. And thus, whatever we face in life, we do not face it alone. He is born not just to kings and queens in palaces, not just in regal, royal places, but in dimly lit back alleys, where we shiver in mangers of sadness or suffering. He comes to us. He finds us in places where Herod and Magi would never think to look. And he lives with us there.

I read an article some time ago about a ten-year-old child who suffered burns over ninety percent of his body. He faced several years of painful procedures and reconstructive surgeries. The doctors learned that when they did what they had to do, he would become incredibly anxious, and his blood pressure would spike to dangerous levels. However, if his mother was in the room, off in a corner so as not to be in their way but remaining in the child's line of sight, he could withstand any procedure without blood pressure incidents. As long as he could see the presence of his mom with him in the pain, he could survive it. Chosen to speak at his college commencement exercises years later, he dedicated his diploma to his mother, who sat in the audience. He said, "She gave me the strength to survive the pain and to embrace the future."

God comes to us in our pain, in our mangers, in our Bethlehem moments. God finds us and stands beside us, giving us the strength to survive the pain and embrace the future. That is the Christmas message. As Matthew puts it, "Jesus was born in Bethlehem . . . ."

Exiting Eden
Genesis 13:1-13, 21-24

Michael B. Brown, senior minister, Marble Collegiate Church, New York, New York.

Page and I visited some church members recently in their new digs in Jersey. After years in a lovely Manhattan apartment, they were ready for trees and a lawn and square footage and auto expenses. So we visited them, and their new home is every bit as beautiful as they described it. It's on a cul-de-sac with a spacious green yard (even a picket fence). From the upstairs bedroom window you can see sailboats moving slowly up the river. At one point during the evening, the husband said, "My wife is so happy with this place that she told me when we die, I can go to heaven if I choose, but she'd just as soon stay in this house!"

Apparently that wife has found her Eden. From a real estate point of view, that's a beautiful thing. But from a biblical point of view, Eden is more elusive. It isn't that we don't find it from time to time. It's just that for whatever reasons, we rarely opt to stay there.

The creation story in Genesis is the attempt of a gifted right-brained religious writer to explain the inexplicable: how this wonderful world came to be, and why we tend so often to make a mess of it. If you read the story as history, you simply wind up in the midst of a pointless debate. If, however, you read the story in a deeper way (seeking not for data but rather for truth), then this ancient tale is a mirror in which we see life in general and ourselves in particular.

There's an old tale about Adam's children, quite some time after exiting Eden. They ask him, "Dad, why did we leave that beautiful place?" Adam answers, "Because your mom ate us out of house and home." After the chuckling subsides, we realize that is not bad exegesis—either from the standpoint of what transpired or how Adam chose to describe it. He just carefully omitted the fact that he along with his wife ate the family out of the garden.

You know the story. God gives Adam and Eve everything . . . life, love, companionship, food, safety, home, peace. God only asks that they do not forget Whose they are—that they do not try to elevate themselves into God's place. But humanity has always done that, as this story implies. We have always put our desires ahead of God's calling. That's what Luther described as "original sin" (*hubris*)—the temptation to place self in the center, nudging God and neighbor out to the periphery. So Adam and Eve eat the forbidden apple ("the fruit of the tree of the knowledge of good and evil," the fruit which they thought would make them as wise and powerful as God). Of course, however hard we try, our efforts to exaggerate the importance of self always fall short. Most folks who are self-absorbed wind up, at best, looking laughable and, at worst, destroying the very self they sought to elevate. Adam and Eve did both.

So back to the punch line: "Your mom ate us out of house and home." When cornered with no way out, when caught red-handed, Adam sought to deflect blame from himself to anybody else in the room, which pretty effectively narrowed it down to three other characters. First, there was the serpent, representing whatever it is that tempts us to make a god of self. But temptation is not the issue, is it? The issue is what we do when temptation comes. Mae West used to say, "When faced with various temptations, I always pick one I haven't tried before." Adam and Eve got on board that train. It was obvious what direction they took when temptation came. Adam simply tried not to share the blame, which belonged equally to him and Eve. He sought instead to deflect, to justify himself by accusing others. And he did it with abandon, starting by pointing a finger at the serpent.

Since the serpent was not really the issue, Adam then turned to Eve. He said to God, "This woman . . . made me eat of the fruit." Really? How about that? Apparently "this woman" was a pretty overpowering character. Adam's testimony makes it sound as if she physically forced him, as if he were tackled and restrained and she shoved the apple in his mouth. Eve, the linebacker. Eve, the professional wrestler. Adam, the wimp. "It's Eve's fault. I didn't want to eat that fruit. I don't even like apples. This woman . . . made me do it."

And when that didn't work, Adam went even further. It wasn't just "this woman" who was guilty. Did you hear the language when we read the lesson? Adam said to God, "This woman who *you* gave me" made me do it. In other words, "God, you share the blame for this. You have complicity. If you hadn't sent Eve down here, I wouldn't be in this mess! It's your fault." That ancient writer understood human nature pretty well. How often do we still attempt to blame God for our poor decisions? Theodicy cannot be explained completely by referring to the unwise choices we make and their inevitable consequences. But most of the time when people shake their fists toward heaven and cry out, "My God, my God, why?" the suffering they endure is not really a random act of nature. Much of the time, as the Bible warns, we do in fact reap what we ourselves have sown. It is understandable to be angry at God when serious illness stands at your doorstep. But if you have abused your body for years and years prior to that illness, is God really the culprit? It is understandable when a spouse walks away to ask God why we mere mortals have to endure such heartbreaks. But if you have been unkind, unloving, or unfaithful long enough, is it really God's fault that the marriage crumbled? Okay, the theodicy question is for another day. But for this day, just know that Adam was not mature enough to accept responsibility for his own decisions, so instead he tried to project blame on others, even on God. "This woman who *you* gave me . . ."

The story teaches, though, that the biblical principle is correct: we really do tend to reap what we have sown. Life has a sense of justice. So Adam and Eve lose Eden. They are sent out, due to their own choices, into a world of fear, and pain, and frustration, and loss, and sickness, and guilt. And there's no turning back. They are no longer protected. Instead, they step face-first into what we call "life." But out there in life, amid all the pains and pitfalls, there are also beauties and blessings. Put another way, we believe that whereas life has a sense of justice, life with God has an even greater sense of grace. Isn't that what Paul was getting at when he wrote, "Where sin increased, grace increased all the more"? (Rom 5:20) Isn't that a central truth of the incarnation? "His name shall be called Immanuel, which means 'God with us.'" (Mt 1:23). Despite the fact that we sometimes reap the inevitable consequences of the unwise seeds we have sown, there is a presence (an unseen strength) that faces life at our side. Grace.

Carlyle Marney was one of the great preachers of the twentieth century, kind of the South's version of our city's Harry Emerson Fosdick. Years ago I heard Dr. Marney weave his account of the Garden story in a sermon he preached at a beautiful place called Lake Junaluska.

Marney said there are three ways to portray God in the story: as dictatorial parent, as permissive parent, or as loving parent. As the first, God lays down the law, explaining clearly the consequence of disobedience. "Eat the apple, get thrown out of the garden, no questions asked." Upon finding apple cores littering the property, God's big voice boomed out: "What is the meaning of this?" Adam and Eve, God's disobedient children, cowered before their angry parent. "You knew the rules," God shouts, "and you broke them. Now pay the consequences. Get out!" Trembling, Adam and Eve take their little suitcases in their hands. And the iron gates of Eden slam shut behind them, and their tears fall in the dust.

In the second portrayal, as permissive parent, God explains to Adam and Eve that everything they want is theirs . . . with one exception. "There's this one tree," God says. "I've tended it and nurtured it, and I really hope you will not touch it. It's very fragile. But everything, I mean everything, else is yours." Adam and Eve consult and decide they will not accept that strictness, so they eat the apples. Upon finding out, God says to them, "Perhaps I didn't make myself clear. It's my fault. I didn't communicate adequately." Adam and Eve answer, "Oh, you communicated clearly. We just don't accept your rules, your regulations, your restrictions. We want to taste freedom. We don't like it here." The two of them storm out in search of a place where they can play by their own rules. And when the iron gates of Eden slam shut, God's tears fall in the dust.

Finally, said Marney, there is a third way of interpreting God from the Garden story: as loving parent. As with the first two renderings, a rule is established ("Do not eat of the fruit of that tree") and a rule is broken. God confronts Adam and Eve and reminds them of the consequences of their choice. They must now leave Eden, entering a world where dangers lurk around every corner. There will be blessings, to be sure, but also suffering. They will hurt, they will weep, they will grieve, they will long for the safety of Eden, but that safety will no longer be found. As I said, we call it "life," and it is not always an easy journey. So Adam and Eve take their suitcases and walk out of the garden. They stand there feeling very much alone and afraid. They dare not raise their eyes to the threatening landscape beyond the garden. They shudder when they hear the iron gates of Eden slam shut behind them. But then, said Marney, they each feel an arm wrap 'round their shoulders. They raise their eyes to an unexpected presence standing between them. And the voice of their loving Parent says, "Well, let's get going."

Whatever we face on the far side of Eden . . . whatever pains or problems are there, whether or not of our own making . . . whatever causes us to shudder with fear or apprehension . . . we do not face it alone. That's what *grace* means. That's what *incarnation* means. "His name shall be called Immanuel—God with us." When the iron gates of safety or security slam shut behind us and we face what has to be faced in life, the gentle arms of a loving Parent wrap around our shoulders. And a strong and kind voice says, "Well, let's get going."

Other available titles from

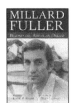

Beyond the American Dream
Millard Fuller

In 1968, Millard finished the story of his journey from pauper to millionaire to home builder. His wife, Linda, occasionally would ask him about getting it published, but Millard would reply, "Not now. I'm too busy." This is that story. *978-1-57312-563-5 272 pages/pb* **$20.00**

The Black Church
Relevant or Irrelevant in the 21st Century?
Reginald F. Davis

The Black Church contends that a relevant church struggles to correct oppression, not maintain it. How can the black church focus on the liberation of the black community, thereby reclaiming the loyalty and respect of the black community? *978-1-57312-557-4 144 pages/pb* **$15.00**

Blissful Affliction
The Ministry and Misery of Writing
Judson Edwards

Edwards draws from more than forty years of writing experience to explore why we use the written word to change lives and how to improve the writing craft. *978-1-57312-594-9 144 pages/pb* **$15.00**

Bottom Line Beliefs
Twelve Doctrines All Christians Hold in Common (Sort of)
Michael B. Brown

Despite our differences, there are principles that are bedrock to the Christian faith. These are the subject of Michael Brown's *Bottom Line Beliefs*. *978-1-57312-520-8 112 pages/pb* **$15.00**

Christian Civility in an Uncivil World
Mitch Carnell, ed.

When we encounter a Christian who thinks and believes differently, we often experience that difference as an attack on the principles upon which we have built our lives and as a betrayal to the faith. However, it is possible for Christians to retain their differences and yet unite in respect for each other. It is possible to love one another and at the same time retain our individual beliefs.

978-1-57312-537-6 160 pages/pb **$17.00**

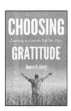

Choosing Gratitude
Learning to Love the Life You Have
James A. Autry

Autry reminds us that gratitude is a choice, a spiritual—not social—process. He suggests that if we cultivate gratitude as a way of being, we may not change the world and its ills, but we can change our response to the world. If we fill our lives with moments of gratitude, we will indeed love the life we have. *978-1-57312-614-4 144 pages/pb* **$15.00**

Contextualizing the Gospel
A Homiletic Commentary on 1 Corinthians
Brian L. Harbour

Harbour examines every part of Paul's letter, providing a rich resource for those who want to struggle with the difficult texts as well as the simple texts, who want to know how God's word—all of it—intersects with their lives today. *978-1-57312-589-5 240 pages/pb* **$19.00**

Dance Lessons
Moving to the Beat of God's Heart
Jeanie Miley

Miley shares her joys and struggles a she learns to "dance" with the Spirit of the Living God. *978-1-57312-622-9 240 pages/pb* **$19.00**

The Disturbing Galilean
Essays About Jesus
Malcolm Tolbert

In this captivating collection of essays, Dr. Malcolm Tolbert reflects on nearly two dozen stories taken largely from the Synoptic Gospels. Those stories range from Jesus' birth, temptation, teaching, anguish at Gethsemane, and crucifixion. *978-1-57312-530-7 140 pages/pb* **$15.00**

Divorce Ministry
A Guidebook
Charles Qualls

This book shares with the reader the value of establishing a divorce recovery ministry while also offering practical insights on establishing your own unique church-affiliated program. Whether you are working individually with one divorced person or leading a large group, *Divorce Ministry: A Guidebook* provides helpful resources to guide you through the emotional and relational issues divorced people often encounter.

978-1-57312-588-8 156 pages/pb **$16.00**

The Enoch Factor
The Sacred Art of Knowing God
Steve McSwain

The Enoch Factor is a persuasive argument for a more enlightened religious dialogue in America, one that affirms the goals of all religions—guiding followers in self-awareness, finding serenity and happiness, and discovering what the author describes as "the sacred art of knowing God." 978-1-57312-556-7 256 pages/pb **$21.00**

Faith Postures
Cultivating Christian Mindfulness
Holly Sprink

Sprink guides readers through her own growing awareness of God's desire for relationship and of developing the emotional, physical, spiritual postures that enable us to learn to be still, to listen, to be mindful of the One outside ourselves. 1-978-57312-547-5 160 pages/pb **$16.00**

The Good News According to Jesus
A New Kind of Christianity for a New Kind of Christian
Chuck Queen

In *The Good News According to Jesus*, Chuck Queen contends that when we broaden our study of Jesus, the result is a richer, deeper, healthier, more relevant and holistic gospel, a Christianity that can transform this world into God's new world.
978-1-57312-528-4 216 pages/pb **$18.00**

Healing Our Hurts
Coping with Difficult Emotions
Daniel Bagby

In *Healing Our Hurts*, Daniel Bagby identifies and explains all the dynamics at play in these complex emotions. Offering practical biblical insights to these feelings, he interprets faith-based responses to separate overly religious piety from true, natural human emotion. This book helps us learn how to deal with life's difficult emotions in a redemptive and responsible way. 978-1-57312-613-7 144 pages/pb **$15.00**

Hope for the Thinking Christian
Seeking a Path of Faith through Everyday Life
Stephen Reese

Readers who want to confront their faith more directly, to think it through and be open to God in an individual, authentic, spiritual encounter will find a resonant voice in Stephen Reese.
978-1-57312-553-6 160 pages/pb **$16.00**

Hoping Liberia
Stories of Civil War from Africa's First Republic
John Michael Helms

Through historical narrative, theological ponderings, personal confession, and thoughtful questions, Helms immerses readers in a period of political turmoil and violence, a devastating civil war, and the immeasurable suffering experienced by the Liberian people.

978-1-57312-544-4 208 pages/pb **$18.00**

A Hungry Soul Desperate to Taste God's Grace
Honest Prayers for Life
Charles Qualls

Part of how we *see* God is determined by how we *listen* to God. There is so much noise and movement in the world that competes with images of God. This noise would drown out God's beckoning voice and distract us. We may not sense what spiritual directors refer to as the *thin place*—God come near. Charles Qualls's newest book offers readers prayers for that journey toward the meaning and mystery of God.

978-1-57312-648-9 152 pages/pb **$14.00**

James (Smyth & Helwys Annual Bible Study series)
Being Right in a Wrong World
Michael D. McCullar

Unlike Paul, who wrote primarily to congregations defined by Gentile believers, James wrote to a dispersed and persecuted fellowship of Hebrew Christians who would soon endure even more difficulty in the coming years.

Teaching Guide 1-57312-604-5 160 pages/ pb **$14.00**

Study Guide 1-57312-605-2 96 pages/pb **$6.00**

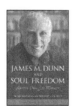

James M. Dunn and Soul Freedom
Aaron Douglas Weaver

James Milton Dunn, over the last fifty years, has been the most aggressive Baptist proponent for religious liberty in the United States. Soul freedom—voluntary, uncoerced faith and an unfettered individual conscience before God—is the basis of his understanding of church-state separation and the historic Baptist basis of religious liberty.

978-1-57312-590-1 224 pages/pb **$18.00**

To order call **1-800-747-3016** or visit **www.helwys.com**

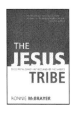

The Jesus Tribe
Following Christ in the Land of the Empire
Ronnie McBrayer

The Jesus Tribe fleshes out the implications, possibilities, contradictions, and complexities of what it means to live within the Jesus Tribe and in the shadow of the American Empire.

978-1-57312-592-5 *208 pages/pb* **$17.00**

Joint Venture
Jeanie Miley

Joint Venture is a memoir of the author's journey to find and express her inner, authentic self, not as an egotistical venture, but as a sacred responsibility and partnership with God. Miley's quest for Christian wholeness is a rich resource for other seekers.

978-1-57312-581-9 *224 pages/pb* **$17.00**

Let Me More of Their Beauty See
Reading Familiar Verses in Context
Diane G. Chen

Let Me More of Their Beauty See offers eight examples of how attention to the historical and literary settings can safeguard against taking a text out of context, bring out its transforming power in greater dimension, and help us apply Scripture appropriately in our daily lives.

978-1-57312-564-2 *160 pages/pb* **$17.00**

Looking Around for God
The Strangely Reverent Observations of an Unconventional Christian
James A. Autry

Looking Around for God, Autry's tenth book, is in many ways his most personal. In it he considers his unique life of faith and belief in God. Autry is a former Fortune 500 executive, author, poet, and consultant whose work has had a significant influence on leadership thinking.

978-157312-484-3 *144 pages/pb* **$16.00**

Maggie Lee for Good
Jinny and John Hinson

Maggie Lee for Good captures the essence of a young girl's boundless faith and spirit. Her parents' moving story of the accident that took her life will inspire readers who are facing loss, looking for evidence of God's sustaining grace, or searching for ways to make a meaningful difference in the lives of others.

978-1-57312-630-4 *144 pages/pb* **$15.00**

To order call **1-800-747-3016** or visit **www.helwys.com**

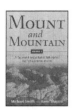

Mount and Mountain
Vol. 1: A Reverend and a Rabbi Talk About the Ten Commandments

Rami Shapiro and Michael Smith

Mount and Mountain represents the first half of an interfaith dialogue—a dialogue that neither preaches nor placates but challenges its participants to work both singly and together in the task of reinterpreting sacred texts. Mike and Rami discuss the nature of divinity, the power of faith, the beauty of myth and story, the necessity of doubt, the achievements, failings, and future of religion, and, above all, the struggle to live ethically and in harmony with the way of God. *978-1-57312-612-0 144 pages/pb* **$15.00**

Overcoming Adolescence
Growing Beyond Childhood into Maturity

Marion D. Aldridge

In *Overcoming Adolescence*, Marion Aldridge poses questions for adults of all ages to consider. His challenge to readers is one he has personally worked to confront: to grow up *all the way*—mentally, physically, academically, socially, emotionally, and spiritually. The key involves not only knowing how to work through the process but also how to recognize what may be contributing to our perpetual adolescence.

978-1-57312-577-2 156 pages/pb **$17.00**

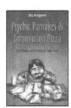

Psychic Pancakes & Communion Pizza
More Musings and Mutterings of a Church Misfit

Bert Montgomery

Psychic Pancakes & Communion Pizza is Bert Montgomery's highly anticipated follow-up to *Elvis, Willie, Jesus & Me* and contains further reflections on music, film, culture, life, and finding Jesus in the midst of it all. *978-1-57312-578-9 160 pages/pb* **$16.00**

Reading Job (Reading the Old Testament series)
A Literary and Theological Commentary

James L. Crenshaw

At issue in the Book of Job is a question with which most all of us struggle at some point in life, "Why do bad things happen to good people?" James Crenshaw has devoted his life to studying the disturbing matter of theodicy—divine justice—that troubles many people of faith.

978-1-57312-574-1 192 pages/pb **$22.00**

Reading Samuel (Reading the Old Testament series)
A Literary and Theological Commentary
Johanna W. H. van Wijk-Bos

Interpreted masterfully by preeminent Old Testament scholar Johanna W. H. van Wijk-Bos, the story of Samuel touches on a vast array of subjects that make up the rich fabric of human life. The reader gains an inside look at leadership, royal intrigue, military campaigns, occult practices, and the significance of religious objects of veneration.

978-1-57312-607-6 *272 pages/pb* **$22.00**

The Role of the Minister in a Dying Congregation
Lynwood B. Jenkins

In *The Role of the Minister in a Dying Congregation* Jenkins provides a courageous and responsible resource on one of the most critical issues in congregational life: how to help a congregation conclude its ministry life cycle with dignity and meaning.

978-1-57312-571-0 *96 pages/pb* **$14.00**

Sessions with Philippians (Session Bible Studies series)
Finding Joy in Community
Bo Prosser

In this brief letter to the Philippians, Paul makes clear the centrality of his faith in Jesus Christ, his love for the Philippian church, and his joy in serving both Christ and their church.

978-1-57312-579-6 *112 pages/pb* **$13.00**

Sessions with Samuel (Session Bible Studies series)
Stories from the Edge
Tony W. Cartledge

In these stories, Israel faces one crisis after another, a people constantly on the edge. Individuals such as Saul and David find themselves on the edge as well, facing troubles of leadership and personal struggle. Yet, each crisis becomes a gateway for learning that God is always present, that hope remains.

978-1-57312-555-0 *112 pages/pb* **$13.00**

Silver Linings
My Life Before and After Challenger 7
June Scobee Rodgers

We know the public story of *Challenger 7*'s tragic destruction. That day, June's life took a new direction that ultimately led to the creation of the Challenger Center and to new life and new love. Her story of Christian faith and triumph over adversity will inspire readers of every age.

978-1-57312-570-3 *352 pages/hc* **$28.00**

Spacious
Exploring Faith and Place
Holly Sprink

Exploring where we are and why that matters to God is an incredible, ongoing process. If we are present and attentive, God creatively and continuously widens our view of the world, whether we live in the Amazon or in our own hometown.

978-1-57312-649-6 156 pages/pb **$16.00**

This Is What a Preacher Looks Like
Sermons by Baptist Women in Ministry
Pamela Durso, ed.

In this collection of sermons by thirty-six Baptist women, their voices are soft and loud, prophetic and pastoral, humorous and sincere. They are African American, Asian, Latina, and Caucasian. They are sisters, wives, mothers, grandmothers, aunts, and friends.

978-1-57312-554-3 144 pages/pb **$18.00**

To Be a Good and Faithful Servant
The Life and Work of a Minister
Cecil Sherman

This book offers a window into how one pastor navigated the many daily challenges and opportunities of ministerial life and shares that wisdom with church leaders wherever they are in life—whether serving as lay leaders or as ministers just out of seminary, midway through a career, or seeking renewal after many years of service. 978-1-57312-559-8 208 pages/pb **$20.00**

Transformational Leadership
Leading with Integrity
Charles B. Bugg

"Transformational" leadership involves understanding and growing so that we can help create positive change in the world. This book encourages leaders to be willing to change if *they* want to help transform the world. They are honest about their personal strengths and weaknesses, and are not afraid of doing a fearless moral inventory of themselves.

978-1-57312-558-1 112 pages/pb **$14.00**

Written on My Heart
Daily Devotions for Your Journey through the Bible
Ann H. Smith

Smith takes readers on a fresh and exciting journey of daily readings of the Bible that will change, surprise, and renew you.

978-1-57312-549-9 288 pages/pb **$18.00**

When Crisis Comes Home
Revised and Expanded

John Lepper

The Bible is full of examples of how God's people, with homes grounded in the faith, faced crisis after crisis. These biblical personalities and families were not hopeless in the face of catastrophe—instead, their faith in God buoyed them, giving them hope for the future and strength to cope in the present. John Lepper will help you and your family prepare for, deal with, and learn from crises in your home. *978-1-57312-539-0 152 pages/pb* **$17.00**

Cecil Sherman Formations Commentary
Add the wit and wisdom of Cecil Sherman to your library. He wrote the Smyth & Helwys Formations Commentary for 15 years; now you can purchase the 5-volume compilation covering the best of Cecil Sherman from Genesis to Revelation.

Vol. 1: Genesis–Job   *1-57312-476-1 208 pages/pb* **$17.00**

Vol. 2: Psalms–Malachi   *1-57312-477-X 208 pages/pb* **$17.00**

Vol. 3: Matthew–Mark   *1-57312-478-8 208 pages/pb* **$17.00**

Vol. 4: Luke–Acts   *1-57312-479-6 208 pages/pb* **$17.00**

Vol. 5: Romans–Revelation   *1-57312-480-X 208 pages/pb* **$17.00**

Made in the USA
Charleston, SC
05 April 2013